# Quiz Me On The Torah

## by
## Dr. Moshe Avital

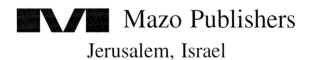 Mazo Publishers

Jerusalem, Israel

Quiz Me On The Torah

Text Copyright © 2007 Dr. Moshe Avital

ISBN: 978-965-7344-17-0

*Published by:*
Mazo Publishers
Chaim Mazo, Publisher
P.O. Box 36084
Jerusalem, Israel 91360

www.mazopublishers.com
Email: info@mazopublishers.com

United States: 1-815-301-3559
Israel: 054-7294-565

# Dedication

May this book become a vehicle of Torah study for Jewish children and youth in the USA and throughout the world. The riches inherent in the Torah are infinite, and those who will study from this book will be motivated to broaden and deepen their knowledge of the Bible, and in turn, enrich and elevate their lives.

I wish to express profound gratitude and thanks to my good friend Naftali Deutsch and his sons Lawrence M., Benjamin A., Andrew M., and Zachary I. for their noble gesture and generosity in making possible the publication of this important volume.

Naftali Deutsch lived through the Shoah and then made his way to Israel where he participated in the War of Liberation. He then went to America and settled in California where he became a very successful builder and businessman. Naftali personifies the unique qualities of Carpathian Jewry in Czechoslovakia. In the new world, he nurtured and raised his children to be sensitive to the needs of the Jewish community and the needs of people in general.

Naftali's four sons graduated from Hillel Hebrew Academy in Los Angeles and from Pepperdine University where they earned their law degrees. Their children continue the family tradition by attending the Stephen S. Wise Day School.

I dedicate this publication of *Quiz Me On The Torah* to Naftali Deutsch, his sons, and their families. Their kindness and chessed toward family, friends, community, and the Jewish people are their hallmark.

Dr. Moshe Avital
January 2007 (Shvat 5767)

# Table Of Contents

## Quiz Me On The Book Of Numbers

## Quiz Me On The Book Of Deuteronomy

# Answers And Sources

## Answers And Sources For The Questions On The Book Of Genesis

# Author's Preface

In an age when the world is groping so desperately toward more adequate forms of spiritual guidance, it is important for modern Jews to study the lessons in our Torah treasure. The Torah is the shining star of the Jewish people, the "guiding light" by means of which we regain our sense of direction whenever events have led us into the wilderness of spiritual unrest and uncertainty.

As a survivor of the Holocaust (Shoah), I can attest that during trying moments when I was in great danger, certain passages from the Torah, about Redemption and of God's promises to the Jewish people, gave me courage, and strengthened my resolve to overcome the atrocities.

It is written in the Torah, "Moses commanded us the Torah, an inheritance of the Congregation of Jacob." (Deut. 33:4) In Ethics of the Fathers, Rabbi Yossi says, "What you have inherited from your father, you must first earn for yourself before you call it yours.

"Prepare yourself for the study of Torah, since the knowledge of it is not an inheritance of yours," (2:17) because the actual knowledge may only be acquired by personal effort.

The Psalmist states that Torah learning brings joy and helps the student to absorb the contents of the subject: "O how I love your teaching, it is my study all day long." (119:97) King David also says that the study of Torah refreshes and fortifies a person's spirit: "The Torah is perfect. It refreshes and restores the soul." (19:8)

My goal with this book is to provide a tool for today's Jewish youth to easily acquire the knowledge Rabbi Yossi refers to. The book is structured to ask very detailed questions and provide the answers and the sources for further research in an exciting and challenging format.

This book is also designed to be a complete study guide for students who are preparing for the International Bible Contest, "Chidon HaTanach" in Hebrew. For 12 years, I had the privilege of administering the International Bible Contest for the World Zionist Organization, and as such, developed more than 1,200 questions and answers, which when known, will fulfill Rabbi Yossi's directive and adequately prepare the contestant. I urge educators and parents to utilize the unique methods of teaching Torah presented in this book in order to challenge your students and children to attain the highest level of Torah knowledge possible.

I hope that this book will raise the interest in Torah study and will serve as a unifying factor for families and groups to learn and discuss Torah issues and points on Shabbat, holidays, and throughout the year.

# About The Author

Dr. Moshe Avital was born Moshe Doft in Bilke, a village in the eastern part of the former Czechoslovakia called Ruthenia, now Ukraine. Brought up in a traditional Jewish home and in a Jewish environment, he received his early secular education in the Czech public school system and his Jewish education in the Jewish schools in his hometown.

At 14, Avital and his family were expelled from Bilke to the Ghetto Beregszasz. The Germans separated him from his family after they were deported to the Auschwitz Concentration Camp where his parents and many siblings were murdered. He was imprisoned as a slave laborer in five other concentration camps before being liberated from Buchenwald by the U.S. Army on April 11, 1945.

In July 1945, Avital joined the Aliyah Bet movement, which was an illegal immigration to Palestine, conducted by the Jewish Brigade of Palestine. He was taken to a secret port in France where he boarded a freight boat which was renamed Yaldei Buchenwald, the Children of Buchenwald. The ship was intercepted by the British Navy, ordered to the Haifa port, where he was forcefully removed from the ship and escorted to Atlit, a detention camp near Haifa. He was liberated one night by members of the Hagannah, a Jewish military underground in Palestine.

Avital later joined the Hagannah and was fully mobilized after the United Nations passed a resolution to partition Palestine. He fought in the War of Liberation, 1947-1950, mostly in the Jerusalem area. He also fought in the 1956 war and served in the Israeli Army. In November 1950, he first came to the United States for his sister's wedding, who had also survived the Holocaust. It was on this trip that he first met Anita Hershman, who later became his wife.

Dr. Avital pursued his higher academic and Judaic studies at Yeshiva University where he graduated with honors and received a B.A., M.S. and Ph.D. in Hebrew Literature.

Dr. Avital is a steady contributor to the Hebrew Press in America and in Israel. He writes about the Holocaust, Israel, Zionism, Jewish Education, American Jewry, Commentaries on the Bible and Jewish Prayers, on Jewish personalities and Jewish Holidays. He speaks half a dozen languages and is a translator. He has translated 10 ancient Hebrew Kabbalah books into English.

Dr. Avital was the official Hebrew to English translator for the ABC Network during the proceedings of Egyptian President Anwar Sadat's historic visit to Israel and the proceedings in the Israeli Knesset, the Parliament, on November 18, 1977, and later on the press conference at the reciprocal trip to Alexandria, Egypt, by Israeli Prime Minister Menachem Begin.

Dr. Avital and his wife, who have three married daughters and eleven grandchildren, live in New York.

# Quiz Me On The Book Of Genesis

Sources and answers to this section begin on page 104

## Multiple Choice Questions

1. Abraham bought the Cave of Machpelah from Ephron the Hittite for:
a. 100 shekels of silver
b. 100 pieces of money
c. 400 pieces of silver
d. 400 zuzim

2. Do you remember who ran away from her mistress?
a. Zilpah from Leah
b. Bilhah from Rachel
c. Hagar from Sarah
d. Deborah from Rebecca

3. Cain killed Abel. Which other brother feared his brother might kill him?
a. Ishmael – Isaac
b. Joseph – Simeon
c. Jacob – Esau
d. Esau – Jacob

4. Lo, it is yet high day (high noon), neither is it time that the cattle should be gathered together, was said to the shepherds by:
a. Joseph      b. Jacob            c. Abraham      d. Isaac

5. Besides Noah, who else, according to the Torah, "walked with God?"
a. Abraham      b. Isaac            c. Jacob            d. Enoch

6. Who specifically was called a righteous man in the Torah?
a. Abraham      b. Isaac            c. Noah            d. Jacob

7. Who was a hairy man?
a. Esau            b. Jacob            c. Ishmael      d. Judah

8. About whom was it said, "And he shall be wild of a man (a wild man)"?
a. Esau            b. Lot            c. Eliphaz      d. Ishmael

9. What happened on the mountains of Ararat?
a. Jacob prayed there　　　　b. Noah's Ark landed there
c. Laban erected a monument　　d. Abraham took Isaac there as an offering

10. At the end of which day of creation was the following said: And God saw everything that He had made and behold, it was very good.
a. First　　b. Third　　c. Fifth　　d. Sixth

11. Who said the following? You may slay my two sons if I bring him not to you.
a. Isaac　　b. Judah　　c. Reuben　　d. Simeon

12. In Isaac's blessings to Jacob and Esau, which of the following is mentioned?
a. A sword　　b. Dew of heaven　　c. Corn and wine　　d. A yoke

13. Who is the Prophet indicated by the following verse in Genesis? "Now, therefore, give back the man's wife, for he is a Prophet."
a. Isaac　　b. Jacob　　c. Joseph　　d. Abraham

14. Man began "to call upon the name of the Lord" after whose birth?
a. Enosh　　b. Tubal-Cain　　c. Enoch　　d. Noah

15. Who said: "The child (boy) is not (gone), and as for me, whither shall I go?"
a. Hagar　　b. Reuben　　c. Jacob　　d. Joseph

16. Jacob purchased a parcel of ground near the city of:
a. Bethel　　b. Salem　　c. Bethlehem　　d. Shechem

17. In the Book of Genesis, the verse "This thing proceeded (comes) from the Lord; we cannot say to you yes or no (bad or good)" refers to:
a. A severe famine　　b. A flood　　c. A marriage　　d. An unusually good harvest

18. That which Jacob bought for a pot of lentils was:
a. Clothes　　b. A camel　　c. A bracelet　　d. The birthright

19. In his famous dream at Bethel, Jacob saw a:
a. Ladder reaching to the heavens　　b. Wine with three clusters of grapes
c. Cows coming out of the Nile　　d. A basket with baked food

בראשית

20. When Jacob returned to Canaan, he feared Esau would make a war, so he:
a. Armed his servants with spears b. Divided into two camps
c. Asked his father Isaac to help him d. Returned to Laban's house

21. Joseph interpreted the seven lean cows in Pharaoh's dream as signifying:
a. Seven years of plenty b. Trouble
c. Lean meat d. Seven years of famine

22. After marrying Leah, how long did Jacob have to wait to marry Rachel?
a. Six weeks b. Seven days c. Seven years d. Fourteen years

23. The minimum number of righteous men necessary to save Sodom from destruction was:
a. 50 b. 20 c. 10 d. 45

24. Before his death, Jacob made Joseph promise that:
a. He will remain a loyal Jew b. He will educate his sons to be Jews
c. He will bury Jacob in Canaan d. He will mummify Jacob's body

25. The first words Joseph spoke after revealing himself to his brothers were:
a. Be not grieved b. Be not angry with yourselves
c. God sent me before you d. Does my father yet live?

26. Who said the following: "I will be surety for him (stand guarantee); of my hand shall thou require him (I will answer to you for him)."
a. Reuben b. Judah c. Simeon d. Levi

27. Who said the following: "You are spies."
a. Avimelech b. Pharaoh c. Potiphar` d. Joseph

28. Another name for Bethlehem is:
a. Efrat b. Luz c. Kiryath Arba d. Shechem

29. Who said, Lord, will you slay even a righteous nation (innocent people)?
a. Abraham b. Avimelech c. Hagar d. Esau

30. The only food specifically mentioned in Genesis to be stored for the seven years of famine was?
a. Wheat b. Corn c. Rye d. Oats

31. Which of the following pairs does not belong in the group?
a. Good and evil                b. Cold and heat
c. Summer and winter            d. Day and Night

32. The second time Jacob's sons went to see Joseph in Egypt, they brought all the following except:
a. Honey      b. Nuts      c. Grapes           d. Almonds

33. The verse "...and she returned not anymore" refers to?
a. Dinah      b. Eve      c. Tamar            d. A dove

34. The flood "blotted out" all the following except?
a. Men      b. Cattle      c. Fish            d. Fowl of the heaven

35. Pharaoh honored Joseph with all the following except?
a. A gold chain                b. A silver bracelet
c. A signet ring               d. A ride in the second chariot

36. The reason why Pharaoh's dream was doubled was?
a. So it would not be forgotten      b. To frighten Pharaoh
c. To test Joseph's skills           d. To show that it would come true

37. To whom does the following verse refer? "Bring her forth and let her be burnt"
a. Dinah      b. Hagar          c. Tamar            d. Lot's wife

38. Which of Joseph's brothers was not present while he was sold to the Ishmaelites?
a. Simeon      b. Reuben          c. Levi            d. Judah

39. The two sons of Jacob who avenged the assault upon Dinah were?
a. Levi and Reuben                b. Simeon and Levi
c. Simeon and Judah               d. Reuben and Judah

40. Indicate the correct order in which Jacob presented his family to Esau?
a. Handmaidens, Rachel, Leah      b. Rachel, handmaidens, Leah
c. Handmaidens, Leah, Rachel      d. Leah, Rachel, handmaidens

בראשית

41. The number of years that Jacob worked as a shepherd for Laban were?
a. 14　　　　　b. 20　　　　　　　c. 17　　　　　　　d. 24

42. The last child of Jacob to be born in Haran was?
a. Dinah　　　b. Benjamin　　　c. Zebulun　　　d. Joseph

43. Nahor lived in the land of?
a. Egypt　　　b. Aram Naharaim　　c. Seir　　　　d. Gerar

44. Rebecca's father was named?
a. Kemuel　　b. Bethuel　　　　c. Chessed　　　d. Uz

45. The verse "...twelve princes shall he beget and I will make him a great nation" refers to?
a. Ishmael　　b. Esau　　　　　c. Jacob　　　　d. Ephraim

46. Fill in the missing number in this verse: "Thy seed shall be a stranger in a land that is not theirs… And they shall afflict them ...... years."
a. 630　　　　b. 500　　　　　　c. 400　　　　　d. 210

47. All of the following lived in Egypt at some time during their lives except?
a. Abraham　　　b. Isaac　　　c. Jacob　　　　d. Joseph

48. What relationship was Terach to Lot?
a. Father　　　　b. Uncle　　　c. Grandfather　　d. Second cousin

49. The Tower of Babel was built in the land of?
a. Egypt　　　　b. Shinar　　　c. Elam　　　　　d. Gerar

50. The Book of Genesis specifically mentions that at one point in his life, Noah practiced all of the following occupations except?
a. Shipbuilding　　b. Shepherd　　c. Winemaker　　d. Farmer

51. The water of the flood in Noah's time began to decrease at the end of ...... days.
a. 200　　　　　b. 100　　　　c. 150　　　　　d. 40

52. After killing his brother, Cain moved to the land of?
a. Shinar　　　　b. Eden　　　　c. Nod　　　　d. Chavilah

53. "This is now bone of my bones" refers to?
a. Adam          b. Eve          c. Jacob      d. The serpent

54. Complete the following verse: "It is not good that man should be ......"
a. Unhappy        b. Alone      c. Uncomfortable    d. Helpless

55. In the verse, "Seeing that his soul is bound up with the lad's soul," the two souls referred to are?
a. Joseph's and Benjamin's       b. Jacob's and Benjamin's
c. Jacob's and Joseph's         d. Isaac's and Jacob's

56. The number of Jacob's sons who first went down to Egypt to buy food was?
a. 7        b. 9        c. 10        d. 11

57. The number of Jacob's sons who went down to Egypt the second time to buy food was?
a. 7        b. 9        c. 10        d. 11

58. Whose house is referred to in the verse "And there was none of the men of the house there within"?
a. Abraham's       b. Lot's        c. Potiphar's      d. Joseph's

59. Which of the following men did Judah promise Tamar would be her husband.
a. Er         b. Onan       c. Perez       d. Shelah

60. Joseph found his brothers feeding the flock near the city of?
a. Hebron        b. Bethel       c. Dothan       d. Shechem

61. The Book of Genesis records the death of Deborah. Near which city did she die?
a. Sodom       b. Haran       c. Bethlehem      d. Bethel

62. What did Jacob do on the parcel of land that he purchased near the city of Shechem?
a. Dug a well       b. Erected an alter
c. Built a house      d. Buried Deborah

63. In the verse "lest he come and smite me, the mother with the children," he refers to?
a. Lot            b. Ishmael           c. Esau           d. Laban

64. Rachel hid her father's teraphim in the?
a. Tent           b. Ground           c. Wagon           d. Saddle

65. The original name of the place where Jacob had his dream was?
a. Kiryat Arba        b. Beer Sheba        c. Hebron        d. Luz

66. "I will not eat until I have told my errand" was said by?
a. The angel to Abraham        b. Abraham's servant to Lot
c. Abraham's servant to Bethuel      d. Judah to Joseph

67. "A piece of land worth four hundred shekels of silver" refers to a field containing?
a. A cave           b. A vineyard           c. A well      d. An olive grove

68. When Isaac walked with Abraham in the land of Moriah, he carried the:
a. Wood           b. Knife           c. Lamb           d. Rope

69. To whom does this verse refer?
"And an angel of the Lord found her by a fountain of water."
a. Rebecca          b. Rachel          c. Deborah          d. Hagar

70. All of the following were allies in war except:
a. Aner           b. Chedorlaomer      c. Abraham          d. Eshkol

71. Which two husbands claimed that his wife was really his sister?
a. Jacob and Isaac        b. Abraham and Jacob
c. Abraham and Isaac      d. Noah and Lamech

72. The meaning of Babel is:
a. To build     b. To make bricks     c. To confound     d. To cooperate

73. When men began to multiply upon the face of the earth, God decided to limit man's years to?
a. 950           b. 140           c. 120           d. 460

74. Which one of the brothers did Joseph bind before their eyes?
a. Simeon                b. Levi                c. Reuben                d. Judah

75. Which one of the following did not answer, "Here I am"?
a. Adam                b. Abraham                c. Joseph                d. Jacob

76. In the first covenant between God and Abram, what did God say to him?
a. He commanded him concerning the rite of circumcision
b. He informed him that Sarah would give birth to a son
c. He commanded him to take Hagar for a wife
d. That his seed would be strangers in a land and slaves for 400 years.

77. Why did Jacob love Joseph more than his other sons?
a. He was the son of his beloved Rachel      b. He was born in his old age
c. The brothers hated him                d. Joseph told his father all his dreams

78. What was the oath that Joseph made his brothers swear before his death?
a. To bury him in the Cave of Machpelah
b. To place his body in a metal coffin and put him in the Nile
c. To bury him in the land of Goshen
d. To take his remains along with them when they left Egypt

79. The eyes of two people became dim with age. One was Isaac. The other was?
a. Noah        b. Abraham        c. Joseph        d. Israel

80. Which one of the matriarchs was not buried in the Cave of Machpelah?
a. Leah        b. Rachel        c. Sarah        d. Rebecca

81. The boundaries that God promised Abram in the first covenant were from the River of Egypt to the:
a. Salt Sea        b. Sea of Kinneret        c. Jordan River        d. Euphrates River

82. What happened on Mount Gilead?
a. Jacob and Esau departed as friends
b. Abraham and Avimelech made a covenant
c. Jacob wrestled with the angel
d. Laban and Jacob departed as friends

83. "Shall the Judge of the whole earth not do justly." These words were said in connection with what event?
a. The destruction brought on by the Flood
b. The destruction of Sodom and Gomorrah
c. The dream of Avimelech
d. Hagar and Ishmael's expulsion

84. Whom did Jacob send to show the way before him unto Goshen?
a. Reuben      b. Simeon          c. Judah              d. Naphtali

85. When did Jacob wrestle with the Angel who changed his name to Israel?
a. On the way to Padan-Aram        b. After Simeon and Levi's violent act
c. When he left Canaan for Egypt       d. After leaving Laban, before seeing Esau

# About Whom Was This Said?

1. He was a cunning hunter, a man of the field.

2. He was the possessor of my house.

3. He was a mighty hunter before the Lord.

4. He was the forger of every cutting instrument of brass and iron.

5. He was of beautiful form and fair to look upon.

6. He had wrought a vile deed in Israel.

7. And the blessing of the Lord was upon all that he had in the house and in the field.

8. For God had made me forget all my toil.

9. And their heart failed them and they turned trembling one to another.

10. For he feared to dwell in Zoar.

11. He was the father of such as dwell in tents and have cattle.

12. His hand shall be against every man and every man's hand against him.

13. The father of the children of Eber.

14. Why do you look so sad today?

15. And let them grow into a multitude in the midst of the earth.

16. (The) father of all such as handle the harp and pipe.

17. He made himself like a stranger and spoke roughly to them.

# Who Did The Following?

1. Who was offered the spoils of battle but refused to take anything?

2. Cursed his grandson that he shall be a slave forever?

3. Who planted a Tamarisk tree and where?

4. Who erected the first monument in memory of the dead and who was it for?

5. And brought forth bread and wine.

6. And he gave him a tenth of all.

# Who Dreamed Of This?

1. Three branches

2. All manner (kinds) of baked goods.

3. A ladder set up on the earth.

בראשית

4. In the simplicity of my heart and the innocence of my hands have I done this.

5. Binding sheaves.

6. Ears, thin and blasted with east wind.

7. Take heed to thyself that you speak not …... either good or bad (beware of saying a single word..

# What Is The Correct Number?

1. How many people were saved from the destruction of Sodom and Gomorrah?

2. How many years did Sarah live?

3. How old was Joseph when he was sold by his brothers?

4. How old was Joseph when he stood before Pharaoh?

5. How many years did Jacob work for Laban?

6. How many shekels did Abraham pay for the Cave of Machpelah?

7. How many people were recorded as having found shelter in Noah's Ark?

8. How old was Isaac when Esau and Jacob were born?

# Identify The Person With The Utensil

1. Silver goblet

2. And I gave the cup into his hand

3. Emptied her pitcher into the trough

4. Took the knife

5. Filled the bottle with water and gave the lad to drink

6. In the uppermost basket there was all manner (kinds) of baked food.

# Who Said This To Whom?

1. "Let us make man in our own likeness, to resemble us."

2. "It is not good for man to be alone, I will make a helper to suit him."

3. "In the sweat of your brow you shall earn your food."

4. "For dust you are and you return to dust."

5. "Am I my brother's keeper?"

6. "You shall be a fugitive and a wanderer over the earth."

7. "My punishment is more than I can bear."

8. "In the clouds I set My rainbow, as a symbol of the covenant between Myself and the earth."

9. "I will make you a great nation and I will bless you and make your name great and you will be a blessing."

10. "Those who bless you, I will bless and anyone who curses you, I will curse them. And in you shall all the families of the earth be blessed."

11. "Let us have no dispute between you and me. If you go to the left, I will go to the right, or, if you go to the right, I will go to the left."

12. "Do not lay hands on the lad, do nothing to him."

13. "Give me to drink, I pray thee, a little water of thy pitcher."

14. "We will call the girl and ask her."

15. Let me swallow, I beg you, some of this red, red, pottage.

16. "God give you dew of heaven and richness of the earth, corn and wine in plenty."

17. "You shall live by the sword and serve your brother."

18. "The Eternal must be here and I never knew it."

19. "I do not deserve all the kindness and loyalty with which you have treated your servant. With staff in hand, I crossed the Jordan River, and now I am two camps."

20. "I am in search of my brothers."

21. "Behold, here is the dreamer."

22. "The boy is gone; whatever is to become of me."

23. "I must make mention of my offering today."

24. "The voice is the voice of Jacob, but the hands are the hands of Esau."

25. "Give me the people and the goods take for thyself."

26. "Deliver me, I pray thee, from the hand of my brother."

27. "What good will it be if we slay our brother and cover up his blood?"

28. "Shall the judge of all the earth not be just."

29. "I will be responsible for him, of my hand shalt thou require him."

30. "Why have you repaid evil for good?"

31. "You shall not take a wife for my son from the daughters of the Canaanites."

32. "Unto thy descendants will I give this land."

תרצשדה

33. "You have striven with human and divine beings and have won?"

34. "Flee to the hills lest you be swept away."

35. "Can I take the place of God?"

36. "And it came to pass as he interpreted to us so it was."

37. "Take heed to thyself that thou speak not to him either good or bad."

38. "Are we not accounted by him strangers? For he hath sold us and hath also quite devoured our price."

39. "Because you are my brother should you therefore serve me for naught?"

40. "You shall call his name Ishmael."

41. "Whoso sheds man's blood, by man, shall his blood be shed."

42. "Has thou but one blessing?"

43. "I will not let you go except if you bless me."

44. "Let me go, for the day breaks."

45. "I had not though to see they face, and lo God hath let me see the seed also."

46. "This heap is a witness between me and thee this day."

47. "Let us not take his life…shed no blood."

48. "Fear not for this also is a son for thee."

49. "I make mention of my faults this day."

50. "Is there yet any portion of inheritance for us in our father's house?"

51. "These men are peaceable with us, therefore let them dwell in the land."

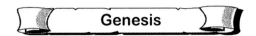

52. "Surely you are my bone and flesh."

# Who Does The Statement Refer To?

1. For thee have I seen righteous before me in this generation.

2. Get thee out of thy country and out of thy birthplace, and out of they father's house.

3. He was a plain man dwelling in tents.

4. This fellow came to settle among us as a stranger, and now he plays the judge.

5. He was a priest of God the Most High.

6. He dwelled in the wilderness and became an archer.

7. The man grew rich and increased his wealth until he became very great.

8. He made himself like a stranger and spoke roughly to them.

9. The angel who hath redeemed me from all evil, bless the lads.

10. By the sword shall thou live.

11. He sowed in the land of Gerar and received in the same year a hundred fold.

12. He shall dwell in the tents of Shem.

13. Cursed be everyone that curses thee.

14. By thee shall Israel bless.

# Who Was The First…?

1. Farmer

2. Shepherd

3. To handle the harp and pipe

4. Forger

5. Matchmaker

6. Oleh

7. Hebrew sent out of Egypt

8. To name the animals and birds

9. Carpenter

10. To be called Israel

11. Who built a city

12. Blacksmith

13. Cheat

14. To plant a vineyard

15. Drunkard

16. Person to be sold as a slave

17. To leave the land of Canaan because of a famine

# Match The Proverb With An Event

1. Do not associate yourself with the wicked; when they are punished, you may be punished with them.

2. A person should always strive to avoid conflicts, since minor quarrels often grow into major combats.

3. He who avoids slander and evil talk about others avoids trouble for himself.

4. A greedy person is eager to get things that do not belong to him.

5. A wise man is careful with his words, for a hasty expression may lead to serious consequences.

6. When your relative or friend is in trouble, do not stand idly by. Go out of your way to help him.

בראשית

7. Do not make boastful promises to others, which you may not be able to keep, say little but do much.

8. A humble and modest person considers himself unworthy of God's blessings and honors bestowed upon him by other men.

9. The religious person always turns toward God for help and guidance.

10. God, who created the world and all its people, shows His mercy, not only to the righteous, but even to the sinners.

# Unique Questions

1. Which of the matriarchs was not buried in the cave of Machpelah and why?

2. Who changed Jacob's name, and what name was he given?

3. What is written in the Torah about each day of creation to support the tradition that, in the Jewish calendar, the day begins in the evening?

4. What is another name for Esau in the Torah?

5. In Jewish custom, a bride covers her face with a veil before going under the Chuppah to be married. Name a bride in the Torah who covered her face with a veil when she saw her husband-to-be from afar.

6. Who did Abraham rescue by going to war?

7. Two women in the Torah are called by the name Deborah. One of them was a Prophetess. Who was the other?

8. Who are described in the Torah as entering in pairs and what did they enter?

9. In which part of Egypt did the Children of Israel live?

10. Name the two sons of Rachel.

11. Mention two people in the Book of Genesis whose names were changed by adding or changing one or two letters?

12. What did Esau receive as the price for his birthright?

13. Who are the two brothers who are each known by another name in additional to their original name?

14. Who was it that "rent his garments and put on sackcloth upon his loins and mourned for his son many days"?

15. Several people in the Torah were given their names before they were born. Mention two of them from the Book of Genesis.

16. Who agreed to marry a man before she had even seen him?

17. What was the name of Joseph's wife?

18. What relation was Laban to Jacob?

19. Who lived longer than anyone else and how old was he when he died?

20. Where was Rachel buried?

21. Three women in the Torah found their future husbands through meetings at a well. Who were the two women in the Book of Genesis.

22. Give another name for each of the following: a. Esau  b. Jacob  c. Joseph

23. Of which non-Jew is it written that "He was priest of God, the Most High"?

24. Name their husbands: a. Keturah  b. Milcha  c. Judith

25. Why is there a tradition or practice among Jews to hold functions on Tuesdays?

26. The number "7" is a significant one in the Torah. List three items or events in the Book of Genesis in which the number "7" plays a role.

27. What is the basis on which the Jewish claim is based in regard to the Land of Israel?

28. How is man's labor described in the Book of Genesis?

29. What is the phrase enjoining mankind to increase its population?

30. For which day of the week does the Torah use the expression, "God saw it was very good."?

31. What kind of animals were used for transportation in Biblical times?

32. What were the laws of Noah which were considered universal laws of morality?

33. Twelve sons and one daughter. Whose family was it and what was the daughter's name?

34. Two brothers tried to save Joseph's life. Who were they and what was their advice?

35. While traveling in a foreign country, two husbands said, concerning their wives, "She is my sister." Who were the husbands and who were the wives?

36. What important events occurred in the following places?
a. Mount Ararat   b. Mount Moriah

37. About whom was the following said?
a. He was a mighty hunter.   b. He was a man of the field.   c. He was a wild man.

38. In the Ethics of the Fathers, it is written: "He who says to another person, 'Mine is mine and thine is mine' is a wicked person". Quote Laban's words to Jacob to show that he was wicked.

39. Who said this to whom? "But his younger brother shall be greater than he..."

40. In Jacob's blessings, he compared some of the traits of these sons to those of what animals?
a. Benjamin   b. Judah   c. Naphtali   d. Dan

41. Who of the patriarchs bought land in Canaan for an everlasting possession? Give their location.

42. What did Joseph say to Benjamin when he met him for the first time in Egypt?

43. What was the former name of each of these places?
a. Bethel   b. Bethlehem   c. Hebron

44. The city of Ai is mentioned in Genesis in connection with what event?

45. In blessing which tribe did Jacob say: "I wait for thy salvation, O Lord..."?

46. What did God promise to Jacob, in the vision at Beer Sheba, before he left the land of Canaan on the way to Egypt?

47. About whom was it said?
a. ...for he is a prophet   b. ...a man with the spirit of God   c. ...a prince of God

48. Name the three tribes that did not receive any blessings from Jacob, but words of censure.

49. Jacob buried two things under the terebinth (oak tree). What were they?

50. To all the brothers, Joseph gave each man changes of raiment, but what two things did he give to Benjamin?

51. Name the mothers of the following people:
a. Ephraim and Menashe   b. Peretz and Zerach   c. Dinah

52. How old were the following when they observed the mitzvah of circumcision?   a. Abraham   b. Isaac   c. Ishmael

53. Who saw the following items in his dreams?
a. Three baskets   b. Goats   c. Sheaves   d. Ears of corn   e. Three twigs

54. The first time the return of our forefathers from a foreign country to their own land was mentioned in the Torah, what was the occasion and what words were said?

55. How did Joseph know that his brothers really regretted that they had sold him into slavery?

56. What two events recorded in Genesis lasted for forty days?

57. When Joseph was asked where he came from, what was his answer?

58. The giving of the tithe (tenth) is mentioned twice in Genesis in connection with what events?

59. When Jacob returned to Canaan and feared his brother Esau would make war with him, what did he do?

60. Name two Israelites who married Egyptian women

## Give The Blessing Jacob Gave To These Sons

1. Joseph

2. Benjamin

3. Dan

4. Zebulun

5. Judah

6. Reuben

7. Naphtali

8. Asher

## Who Were These People?

1. Mamre

2. Malchizedek

3. Phicol

4. Deborah

## Identify These Places

1. Ur of the Chaldees

2. Haran

3. Shechem

4. Kiryat Arba

## What Story Is Connected With The Following?

1. A coat

2. A goblet

3. A mountain

4. A ladder

5. A basket

## In What Events Were These Expressions Used?

1. The threshing floor of Atad.

2. They conspired against him.

3. Savoury food.

4. Unstable as water.

5. His bread shall be fat.

6. An abomination to the Egyptians.

7. What is your occupation?

8. Thou art a prince of God in our midst.

9. Placed east of Eden.

10. Sinew of the thigh-vein.

בראשית

*Worldwide national winners who participated in the Chidon HaTanach contest in Israel at a reception by Israeli President Zalman Shazzar on Yom Hatzmaut 1970.*

*Yaacov Halperin, the coordinator of the contest in Israel is seated first on the left, followed by Dr. Avital, seated second from the left. President Shazzar is seated fourth from the left.*

# Quiz Me On The Book Of Exodus

Sources and answers to this section begin on page 120

## Multiple Choice Questions

1. Why did Pharaoh's daughter save the child from the river?
a. She had no son　　　　　　　　b. She took pity on him
c. She didn't agree with the king's decree　　d. His sister begged her to save him

2. The first mitzvah which the Jews were commanded to observe in Egypt begins with the words:
a. Sanctify unto Me all the first-born
b. This month shall be unto you the beginning of months
c. This is the ordinance of the Passover
d. And it shall be for a sign upon thy hand

3. With what complaint did Moses cry out, "They are almost ready to stone me?"
a. When they received the manna　　　　b. When they stood at the Red Sea
c. When they lacked water　　　　　　　d. When they lacked meat

4. Jethro mentioned several character qualities for the selection of Judges. Which of these qualities was not mentioned?
a. God-fearing　　　　　　　　b. Men of truth
c. Hating unjust gain　　　　　　d. Men of kindness

5. Of the Ten Commandments, which one states a specific reward for its observance?
a. Remember the Sabbath day　　　　b. Thou shalt not covet
c. Honor thy father and thy mother　　d. Thou shalt not bear false witness

שמות

6. What is the law if a man steals a garment later found in his possession?
a. He pays double
b. He just returns the garment
c. He pays four-fold
d. He pays a fine

7. Every person who was remembered in the first census was required to pay a half-shekel from what age upward?
a. Twenty
b. Thirteen
c. Twenty-one
d. Thirty

8. One who slays a person unintentionally can save his life by:
a. Taking hold of the corners of the altar
b. Fleeing to a city of refuge
c. Paying ransom to the avenger of blood
d. Bringing a sacrifice to the temple

9. The reason for the Sabbath as stated in the Ten Commandments is:
a. Because the Lord took the Children of Israel out of Egypt
b. Because God rested on the seventh day
c. Because the Egyptians did not give the Jews a day of rest
d. Because it is good for the body to rest one day a week

10. Which of the following holidays is not a pilgrimage festival?
a. Sukkot        b. Shavuot        c. Rosh Hashanah        d. Passover

11. When a poor man gives his garment as a pledge, when must the lender return it to him?
a. When the money is paid back
b. At the end of three days
c. The same day when the sun goes down
d. No later than a week

12. Of the sons of Jacob, who is not mentioned among those who came with Jacob to Egypt?
a. Judah        b. Joseph        c. Reuben        d. Levi

13. Identify the Egyptian who feared the word of the Lord?
a. He who made his servants and his cattle flee into the houses
b. He who brought sacrifices to the God of Israel
c. He who gave the Israelites vessels of silver and gold
d. He who disobeyed Pharaoh

ש

מ

ו

ת

14. What is to be always on the Table in the Mishkan?
a. The show bread     b. The Menorah
c. The Laver          d. The Ephod

15. In what plague was "fire flashing up" in its midst?
a. Darkness          b. Gnats
c. Locust            d. Hail

16. What did Moses throw heavenward which turned to boils?
a. Soot of the furnace          b. Water of the Nile
c. Sand from Mount Sinai        d. Straw

17. In addition to the plague of darkness, which plague "covered the face of the whole earth, so that the land was darkened"?
a. Gnats             b. Locust
c. Hail              d. Boils

18. About whom is it said: "They saw not one another"?
a. Moses and Aaron    b. The Egyptians
c. The Amalekites     d. Levi's sons

19. About whom is it said: "and slay every man his brother"?
a. The Egyptians     b. Levi's sons
c. The Amalekites    d. The Taskmasters

20. Gerson was the son of?
a. Moses             b. Levi             c. Aaron             d. Joshua

21. Name the animal mentioned in the plague of the first-born?
a. Camel             b. Dog             c. Lamb             d. Donkey

22. In what connection was the term "door post" (not doorposts) mentioned?
a. The sign of blood on the doors          b. The Tefillin
c. When a Hebrew slave does not want to go free     d. The tent of Moses.

23. In which of the Ten Commandments is God's attitude toward those who hate Him and those who love Him expressed?
a. Second            b. Fourth             c. Sixth             d. Tenth

שמות

36

24. The attitude towards the poor is expressed in which law?
a. Neither shall you favor the poor man in his cause
b. Of the best of his field, and of the best of his vineyard, shall he make restitution
c. You shall restore it to him by the time the sun goes down
d. You shall surely bring it back to him again

25. The wood of what tree was the wood used to build the Ark?
a. Fig                 b. Olive
c. Palm                d. Accacia

26. What "firstling" shall you redeem with a lamb, or "break its neck"?
a. Camel        b. Ox          c. Donkey            d. Goat

27. In the Book of Exodus, the first Hebrew month is called?
a. Aviv         b. Ziv         c. Nissan            d. Tishri

28. Which law expresses the attitude towards the enemy's ox or his donkey?
a. You shall restore it to him by the time the sun goes down
b. You shall surely bring it back to him again
c. A stranger shall you not oppress for you were strangers in the land of Egypt
d. You shall not wrest the judgment of the poor in his cause

29. Before the birth of Moses, by what name is his mother mentioned in the Book of Exodus?
a. Jochebed           b. Shifra        c. Daughter of Levi          d. Puah

30. After the child was placed in a basket by the river's bank, who stood from afar to know what would be done to Moses?
a. His mother          b. His sister    c. His brother          d. His father

31. Moses gave several reasons why he did not want to take upon himself God's mission. What is the first reason?
a. "Who am I that I should go unto Pharaoh"
b. " I am not a man of words"
c. "I am slow of speech"
d. "Send by the hand of him whom you will send"

32. Before he left Egypt, Moses took with him the bones of?
a. His parents        b. Judah       c. Joseph       d. Levi

שמות

33. In the Book of Exodus, the Feast of Weeks is called:
a. The Feast of the Harvest
b. The Feast of the Ingathering
c. The Feast of Aviv
d. The Feast of the Tabernacles

34. Two cubits in length, one cubit in breadth and a cubit and a half in height. These were the dimensions of the?
a. Ark      b. Altar of Gold      c. Table in the Tabernacle      d. Altar of Incense

35. Which garment was not worn by the common Priest (Kohen)?
a. Robe    b. Breeches      c. Ephod      d. Tunic

36. On the plate of the High Priest were engraved the words:
a. High Priest                b. Holy to the Lord
c. Anointed of the Lord        d. Servant of the Lord

37. Which tribe did not participate in the sin of the Golden Calf?
a. Judah        b. Simeon      c. Levi        d. Benjamin

38. How did the women participate in the work of the Tabernacle?
a. They baked the show bread
b. They prepared the anointing oil
c. They spun the goat's hair
d. They prepared the incense

39. Which was the first nation that waged war against Israel after leaving Egypt?
a. Edom        b. Ammon            c. Amalek          d. Moab

40. What advice did Jethro give to Moses?
a. Appoint judges
b. Count the people
c. Judge people in the morning only
d. Appoint Aaron and his sons as judges

41. In the Book of Exodus, six of the seven nations who lived in the Promised Land of Canaan are mentioned. Which one is not mentioned?
a. Perizzite    b. Hivite      c. Amorite    d. Girgashite

42. During which plague is this expression used: "Have you this glory over me"?
a. Frogs        b. Swarms of flies      c. Locusts      d. Hail

43. Where is the place the Children of Israel complained about the lack of graves in Egypt?
a. Marah                        b. At the Red Sea
c. The desert of Sin            d. Massah and Meribah

44.  Among the positive traits that Jethro mentioned to Moses in connection with the selection of Judges, which of the following traits was not mentioned?
a. Able men                     b. Men of truth
c. Men of charitable deed       d. Haters of unjust gain

45. Which Commandment teaches us not to be jealous of a neighbor's possessions?
a. Thou shall not steal
b. Honor thy father and mother
c. Thou shall not covet
d. Thou shall not murder

46. When does a bondman gain his freedom?
a. After working seven years
b. After the death of his master
c. After working fifteen years
d. When his master takes out his eye or tooth

47. What is it that Moses burned and gave of its ashes to the Children of Israel to drink?
a. Leavened bread               b. Manna
c. Golden Calf                  d. Quail

48. Why did God not want the Children of Israel living with the nations of Canaan?
a. Because there wasn't enough room in the land for all of them
b. Because the Children of Israel feared them
c. Because they would cause the Children of Israel to sin
d. Because they would get to love one another

49. In the Book of Exodus, we find four words of redemption. What is their correct order?

a. I will redeem;    I will deliver;    I will bring;    I will take

b. I will take;    I will bring;    I will redeem;    I will deliver

c. I will bring;    I will deliver;    I will redeem;    I will take

d. I will deliver;    I will redeem;    I will bring;    I will take

50. What did God command to be kept throughout the generations?

a. The show bread    b. An omerful of manna

c. The quail    d. Double bread

51. What did Moses do as a sign of thanks to God when he was saved from Pharaoh's sword?

a. He prayed and gave thanks to God    b. Named his son Eliezer

c. Gave a tithe    d. Accepted the leadership of the Jewish people

52. How many times its value does one pay for stealing an ox and slaughtering or selling it?

a. Five times    b. Four times    c. Three times    d. Two times

53. Why didn't the Children of Israel listen to Moses when he brought them the news of their redemption?

a. They feared Pharaoh

b. They thought Moses was a dreamer

c. They had despaired of redemption

d. They suffered from impatience of spirit and cruel bondage

54. In connection with which subject is the following said?
"The rich shall give more, and the poor shall not give less."

a. The rich man and the poor man in court    b. The gathering of the manna

c. Priestly gifts    d. The half shekel

55. Why didn't the midwives put the Hebrew children to death?

a. The Hebrews gave them gifts    b. They overlooked Pharaoh's edict

c. Moses commanded them not to kill them    d. They feared God

56. What is the reward promised by God for the observance of the command to honor parents?

a. Riches    b. Good luck (Mazel)    c. Long life    d. A large family

ש

מ

ו

ת

57. When does a Hebrew slave go free?
a. After twenty years      b. During Jubilee
c. After six years      d. After seven years

# Who Did The Following?

1. He hardened his heart and hearkened not to them.

2. She sent her handmaid to fetch it.

3. He fashioned it with a graving tool.

4. He departed not out of the tent.

5. He made a golden crown to the border thereof round about.

6. He rejoiced for all the goodness which the Lord had done to Israel.

7. She took a timbrel in her hand and all the women went after her with timbrels and with dances.

8. They were sent by Moses to sacrifice burnt offerings and peace offerings.

9. The king who fought Israel in Rephidim.

10. His hands were steady until the going down of the sun.

11. Took the veil off.

12. Cut off the foreskin of her son.

13. He sinned yet more.

14. He had straitly sworn of the Children of Israel.

15. He made ready his chariots.

שׁ

מ

ו

ה

# Fill In The Missing Words

1. You shall not follow a ….. to do …..

2. You shall not afflict any ….or ….child.

3. Put not your hand with the … to be an unrighteous …..

4. All that the Lord has spoken, we will ….and …..

5. But all the Children of Israel had …..in their …..

6. And it came to pass, when Moses held up his …..that Israel …….

7. The Lord is my …….and song and He has become my ………

8. Who is like unto …….. O Lord, among the ………

9. You shall be to me a ……….. of Priests and a holy ………..

10. You shall not ………a stranger for you were ………… in the land of Egypt.

11. The Lord ……… the Sabbath day and ………it.

12. You shall not …….. a kid in its mother's …………..

13. And behold the bush ……… with fire and the bush was not ………

14. Take off your …….. from your feet for the place where you stand is …… ground.

15. Let my ……… that they may hold a feast unto Me in the ………

16. One law shall be unto ………… and unto the ……… that dwells among you.

17. When Moses ……… his hand, that ………… prevailed.

18. Of every man whose heart makes him ……… you shall take my ……….

19. It is not the voice of them that shout for ......., neither is it the voice of them that cry for being ........

20. And the Lord showed him a ....... And he cast it into the ..............

21. And I will give you the ....... of stone, and the ........ and the commandment.

22. For a gift blinded them that have ........., and perverted the words of the .........

23. Keep thee .... from a false matter; and the innocent and righteous ....... you not.

## Match The Following Names

1. Second son of Moses

2. Grandfather of Moses

3. Grandson of Aaron

4. Father of Elisheba

5. Assistant to Bezalel

6. Brother of Elisheba

7. Son of Aaron

8. Saved the male children

9. Son of Nun

## What Stories Are Connected With The Following?

1. A basket

2. A rod

3. A drum (timbrel)

4. The eagles

5. A jar

6. A pillar of cloud and pillar of fire

7. A kid (goat)

שׁ

מ

ו

ת

# What Happened At These Places?

1. Mount Horeb        2. Pi-hahiroth        3. Marah

4. Sukkot             5. Goshen

# What Is The Law?

1. If there is born to a man a first-born son?

2. If there is born a firstling to your ass?

3. If your enemies' donkey lies down under his burden?

4. If an ox gores a man or a woman, and they die?

5. If an ox gores a bondman?

# Match The Places

1. Battle of the Amalekites

2. Moses lived there after fleeing Egypt

ש    3. Israel's first stop after leaving Egypt

4. Scene of the Burning Bush

מ    5. Had 70 palm trees

6. Bitter waters that became sweet

ו    7. People complained about bread and meat

ת    8. Southern border of the Land of Israel

9. Northern border of the Land of Israel

# About Whom Or What Was It Said?

1. If they cry at all to Me, I will surely hear their cry.

2. Be not rebellious against him, for he will not pardon your transgression.

3. When he sees you, he will be glad in his heart.

4. Thou shalt restore it to him when the sun goes down.

5. If he came in by himself, he shall go out by himself.

6. There remained not one in all the border of Egypt.

7. The rich shall not give more, and the poor shall not give less.

8. It shall be for frontlets between thine eyes.

9. And it covered the face of the land.

10. And you shall let nothing of it remain until morning.

11. You shall cast it to the dogs.

12. With their faces one to another.

13. He has filled him with the spirit of God.

14. And it returned to its strength when the morning appeared.

15. You shall take him from My altar, that he may die.

16. He shall be your spokesman unto the people.

17. And behold your servants are beaten.

ש

מ

ו

ת

18. And behold it was turned again as his other flesh.

19. Neither shall you make any like it, according to the composition thereof.

20. And it shall become small dust over all the land of Egypt.

21. And it came to pass at even …. and it covered the camp.

22. For they covered the face of the whole earth.

23. And the taste of it was like wafers made with honey.

24. A night of watching.

# Who Said To Whom?

1. And when He seeth thee, He will be glad in His heart.

2. Call Him that He may eat bread.

3. It is the finger of God?

4. Why do you strike your brother?

5. Who made you chief ruler over us?

ש   6. Who said and on what occasion: "This is your God, O Israel who brought you out of the land of Egypt."?

מ   7. Let me go, I pray thee and return unto my brethren that are in Egypt and see whether they be yet alive?

ו   8. You shall provide, out of all the people, able men that fear God, men of truth, hating unjust gain…and let them judge the people at all seasons.

ת   9. (He) delivered us out of the hand of the shepherds, and moreover He drew water for us, and watered the flock.

10. Who is the Lord, that I should harken to his voice?

11. Blot me, I pray thee, out of Your book which You have written.

12. Come let us deal wisely with them, lest they multiply.

13. Whosoever is on the Lord's side, let him come to me

14. Get you unto your burdens.

15. Today you shall not find it in the field.

16. Let no man leave of it until the morning.

17. You shall carry up my bones away hence with you.

18. Because there were no graves in Egypt, hast thou taken us away to die in the wilderness?

19. How long shall this man be a snare unto us.

20. Write this for a memorial in the book.

21. There is a noise of war in the camp.

22. They are entangled in the land.

23. And let them not regard lying words.

24. You will surely wear away, both you and this people.

25. But who are they that shall go?

26. Send, I pray Thee, by the hand of him whom You will send.

27. You are idle, you are idle

ש

מ

ו

ת

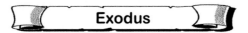
# Unique Questions

1. What is the significance of each of the three major pilgrimage festivals?

2. How did God reveal Himself to Moses?

3. What sustained the Israelites in the desert for forty years?

4. How does the Torah describe the Promised Land?

5. One of the Sabbaths of the year is called Shabbat Shira. Why?

6. Why didn't God lead the Israelites from Egypt directly to the Promised Land?

7. What events in the Book of Exodus deal with the number ten?

8. Who named Moses and why?

9. It burned with fire and was not consumed. What is the reference?

10. "There is no straw given to your servants, and they say to us: Make bricks." What is the reference?

11. According to the Book of Exodus, Moses was "slow of speech." Who was his spokesman?

12. The Torah reminds the Israelites numerous times to treat the stranger and foreigner with kindness and justice. What reason is usually given for this injunction?

13. Who made the "Golden Calf" under the pressure of the people at the foot of Mount Sinai?

14. Who did not eat or drink for 40 days?

15. Which day of the week is a covenant between God and the Jewish people?

16. What phrase characterizes slavery in Egypt?

ש

מ

ו

ת

17. What protected and guided the Israelites during their wanderings in the desert?

18. What is the reference in the Torah to ear piercing?

19. What is the fifth commandment?

20. What is the Biblical source for the eternal light in the synagogue?

21. What expression in the Torah describes the stubbornness of the Jewish people?

22. Which Egyptian cities did the Israelite slaves build?

23. *Naaseh ve-nishma* (We shall do and obey) is a well known expression. Who said it and on what occasion?

24. "Thus shall you eat it … with your loins girded, your shoes on your feet, and your staff in your hand. You shall eat it in haste." Which holiday does this refer to?

25. On Sabbath and Holidays it is customary to place two *Challot* (Sabbath Loaves) at the head of the table. With what Biblical custom is this connected?

26. When Moses fled from Pharaoh, to which land did he go?

27. Who is the child in the following verse? "She opened it and saw it, even the child; and behold a boy that wept, and she had compassion on him."

28. Pharaoh gave instructions to two Hebrew midwives to kill every male child born to Hebrew parents. Who were the midwives?

29. Which religious observance stems from the following verse: "And it shall be for a sign unto thee upon thy hand and for a memorial between thine eyes"?

ש

30. What is the taste of the manna likened to in the Torah?

מ

31. Name the three feasts during which all males are required to "appear before the Lord God"?

ו

32. On which mountain did the Lord first appear to Moses as a burning bush?

ת

33. Where did the Egyptians get drinking water during the first plague?

34. What was the name of Moses' wife?

35. Which land lies on the shortest route from Egypt to the land of Canaan?

36. Which night "is a night of watching unto the Lord for all the Children of Israel throughout these generations"?

37. To whom does this refer to: "And you shall be unto me a kingdom of priests and a holy nation"?

38. How many Israelites left Egypt with Moses?

39. What are the punishments in the Torah for theft?

40. In connection with which crime does the Torah say the following: "Thou shall take him from Mine altar that he may die"?

41. Which plagues were the Egyptians magicians able to bring about?

42. Name the sons of Aaron?

43. By what name did Moses call the tent he pitched outside the camp of the Israelites in the desert?

44. Which non-Jew "rejoiced for all the goodness which the Lord had done to Israel"?

45. According to the Book of Exodus, how long did the Children of Israel dwell in Egypt?

46. How many Hebrews entered Egypt with Jacob and how many left with Moses?

47. When Moses and Aaron first came to Pharaoh they did not ask him to let the Israelites go free. What was their first request?

48. God told Moses to use a certain name to tell the Children of Israel who sent him. What was the name?

49. Why were Aaron and the people of Israel afraid to come near Moses as he descended from Mount Sinai after he received the tablets for the second time?

50. What is the Biblical law if a man dug a pit and did not cover it and a neighbor's ox fell into it and was killed?

51. What is the Biblical reward for honoring one's parents?

52. How was the census of the Hebrews taken in the wilderness?

53. What was written on Aaron's breastplate?

54. Which vegetation was smitten by the plague of hail and which not? Give the reason for each.

55. By what other names are the three pilgrimage festivals of Pesach, Shavuot, and Sukkot called in the Book of Exodus?

56. In the song of Moses, it is stated: "The peoples have heard; they tremble". Which four nations are mentioned there?

57. What four things did Moses do to the Golden Calf?

58. The east wind came to the aid of Israel on two occasions. What were they?

59. Bezalel made the vessels for the Tabernacle. List the first three vessels in their proper order.

60. The dog is mentioned twice in Exodus under what conditions?

61. The first two plagues were brought upon the Egyptians through whom?

62. Moses said: "I have been a stranger in a strange land." Which land is this?

63. Identify these two similar names mentioned in the Book of Exodus; Elazar and Eliezer.

64. Identify who did it and what took place:
"From the morning unto the morning"; "From evening to morning"

ש

מ

ו

ת

65. The Israelites had to keep certain things.
a. What was to be kept for four days?
b. What was to be kept until the morning?
c. What was to be kept "throughout the generations"?

66. Who or what did not remain?
a. There remained not one.
b. There remained not one..in all of Egypt.
c. There remained not so much as one of them.

67. Which two people supported Moses' hands when he was praying for the victory of the Israelites over the Amalakites?

68. Before they left Egypt, the Children of Israel ate the meat of the lamb with two other foods. What were these two foods?

69. Name at least four articles of clothing that the High Priest wore.

70. What were the names of Moses' two sons? Why did he choose these names?

71. Where in the Torah is the prohibition for leavened bread on Passover found?

72. Before they left Egypt, God commanded the Children of Israel to borrow three things from the Egyptians. What are they?

73. On Passover night in Egypt, the Children of Israel were commanded to do everything in haste. Give the four examples of haste.

74. Which work is forbidden on the Sabbath, but allowed on a festival? Show proof from the Book of Exodus.

75. In the song at the Red Sea, Moses compares the drowning or destruction of the Egyptians to three things. What are they?

76. When the High Priest came to minister in the Tent, it is written: "and the sound thereof shall be heard when goeth in unto the holy place." What sound does this refer to?

77. What event took place "on the third day"?

שׁ

מ

ו

ת

# Quiz Me On The Book Of Leviticus

Sources and answers to this section begin on page 134

## Multiple Choice Questions

1. What reason does the Torah give for building a sukkah and dwelling in it?
a. It's the harvest holiday which should be observed in the outdoors
b. Dwelling in the sukkah substitutes offering sacrifices
c. As a remembrance that the Children of Israel dwelled in sukkot in the desert
d. As a substitute for worshipping in the Holy Temple

2. In what month of the year and on what day does the holiday of Passover begin?
a. In the second month on the tenth day
b. In the seventh month on the fifteenth day
c. In the tenth month on the fifteenth day
d. In the first month on the fifteenth day

3. During the harvest, the farmers of Israel were required to leave the corner of the field uncut for:
a. The poor and the stranger   b. The Kohanim      c. The judges      d. The kings

4. Which year is the sabbatical year?
a. The sixth year        b. The seventh year
c. The eighth year       d. The tenth year

5. Why does the Torah prohibit making a slave of our fellow human beings?
a. Because it is forbidden for Jews to have slaves
b. Because slaves were permitted only in the Diaspora and not in the Holy Land
c. Because the Children of Israel are the servants of God
d. Because slaves belong to the Priests

6. The Torah requires that we relate to strangers as though they were our:
a. Brothers      b. Fellow citizens      c. Competitors      d. Servants

7. The Torah commands us not to leave any remnants of sacrifices until the morning. What else are we forbidden to keep until the morning?
a. Burning the eternal light          b. Lighting the menorah
c. Keeping the holy loaves intact      d. Holding back wages of a hired servant

8. While in the desert, who was put in the guardhouse, stoned and why?
a. Miriam, because she turned leprous
b. Korach, because he rebelled against Moses and Aaron
c. One who blasphemed the Lord, because it was unclear how to punish him
d. Eldad and Medad, because they prophesied in the camp

9. Which utensils cannot be cleaned (koshered) and therefore are to be destroyed if they become unclean?
a. Glassware      b. Earthen vessels      c. Silverware      d. Wooden vessels

10. On what year, after planting a tree, are we allowed to eat of its fruit?
a. On the first          b. On the third
c. On the fourth          d. On the fifth

11. The sentence "You shall mortify yourselves" refers to which holiday?
a. Rosh Hashanah      b. Yom Kippur      c. Tisha B'Av      d. Taanit Esther

12. Who is required to dwell in the sukkah?
a. The Kohen  b. The Levi   c. The Israelite   d. All citizens or residents of Israel

13. On which holiday in the Fiftieth Year was the Shofar blown to proclaim the Jubilee?
a. Rosh Hashanah      b. Yom Kippur      c. Sukkot      d. Passover

14. On which festival does the Torah command the Jewish people to rejoice?
a. Passover          b. Shavuot          c. Purim      d. Sukkot

15. What kind of oil was used to light the menorah in the Tabernacle?
a. Fish oil          b. Pure olive oil
c. Oil from a kosher animal   d. Vegetable oil

ו

ה

ק

ר

א

16 The phrase "Shall not be sold in perpetuity" applies to :
a. A maid servant     b. A red heifer
c. Land            d. A woman

17. Whom of the following does the Torah command us not to oppress?
a. A woman       b. Your neighbor
c. The stranger     d. A hired worker

18. The Torah commands us to blow the Shofar on Rosh Hashanah. On what other occasion are we also enjoined to blow the Shofar?
a. Passover       b. Shavuot
c. Sukkot         d. On Yom Kippur which falls in the Jubilee year

19. One of the Ten Commandments is to "Honor your mother and your father." In the Book of Leviticus, this commandment is repeated and precedes another important commandment. What is it?
a. To keep the sabbatical year     b. To keep the Sabbath
c. To love the stranger          d. To care for the poor

20. What kind of writing or imprint does the Torah forbid?
a. Hieroglyphics    b. Cuneiform      c. Tattooing      d. Cursive

21. The distinctions of a kosher animal are:
a. It has fins and scales
b. It parts the hoof, is cloven footed and chews the cud
c. It walks on all fours and hops
d. It eats flesh

22. According to the Torah, people who observe the sabbatical year will be blessed with:
a. Long life               b. Many children
c. An abundant crop in the sixth year    d. Rewards in the world to come

23. Which animal chews its cud but does not have a split hoof?
a. The camel   b. The pig     c. The cow     d. The deer

24. According to the Torah, every field and house returns to its original owner in the jubilee year. To which group of people does this law not apply?
a. Women     b. Judges     c. Prophets     d. Levites

25. What distinguishes a kosher fowl?
a. It walks on all fours
b. All winged things that go upon all fours, which have jointed legs above their feet for leaping upon the ground
c. It walks on two feet
d. It feeds on carrion

26. How did Aaron react to the death of his two sons?
a. He cried bitterly            b. He screamed aloud
c. He complained against God    d. He kept quiet

27. What was brought in the Temple on the "morrow after the seventh week?"
a. A new meal-offering          b. The sacrifice of the Omer
c. The tithe                    d. The show bread

28. According to the Torah, how shall we behave towards the slave (bondman)?
a. As a brother                 b. As a home-born of the land
c. As an enemy                  d. As a slave

29. What is the punishment for one who does not afflict himself of Yom Kippur?
a. He shall be cut off from his people    b. He shall be stoned
c. He pays a fine                         d. He is sent out of the camp

30. Which holy day is referred to in the Torah with the expression, "A memorial proclaimed with the blast of horns"?
a. Yom Kippur            b. Rosh Hashanah
c. The month of Elul     d. A call to war

31. Concerning whom is it said, "You shall not do him wrong"?
a. The murderer     b. The Canaanite     c. The stranger     d. The slave

32. Which holiday is described in the Torah as "A sabbath of solemn rest"?
a. Yom Kippur     b. The Sabbath     c. Rosh Hashanah     d. Passover

33. What are the signs of kosher fish?
a. Chews its cud       b. Cloven-footed
c. Fins and scales     d. Parting the hoof

# Fill In The Missing Words

1. And your threshing shall reach unto the …….. and the vintage shall reach unto the …….. time.

2. You shall not ……. thy brother in thy heart; you shall surely ……. the neighbor.

3. You shall rise up before the ……. head, and honor the face of the ……. man.

4. You shall not curse the ……nor put a stumbling block before the …….

5. And proclaim ……. throughout the land unto all the …….. thereof.

6. You shall do no ……. in judgment, in meteryard, in ……., or in measure.

7. In this year of ……. you shall return every ……. to his possessions.

8. You shall have one manner of …….. as well for the stranger as for the ……..

9. And five of you shall chase a …….., and a hundred of you shall chase ……..

10. And I will give ……. in the land, and you shall lie down and none shall make you ……..

# About What Or Whom Was It Said?

1. And he shall take a wife in her virginity.

2. And they put him in ward.

3. And you shall return every man to his possession.

4. You shall love your neighbor as yourself.

5. You shall love him as yourself.

6. And you shall bring forth the old from before the new.

# To What Or To Whom Is Referred?

1. From evening to evening.

2. From evening to morning.

3. Seven sabbaths of years.

4. Seven weeks.

5. The fruit of goodly trees.

6. And boughs of thick trees.

7. Then I will give your rains in their season.

8. And let all the congregation stone him.

9. As a servant hired year by year shall he be with him.

10. You shall not rule, one over another, with rigor.

# Who Said To Whom?

1. "Draw near, carry your brethren from before the sanctuary out of the camp."

2. "Drink no wine nor strong drink."

# Identify The Person

1. They offered strange fires on the altar.

2. Moses was angry at them.

3. He remained silent when his sons died.

# Unique Questions

1. What Biblical phrase is inscribed on the Liberty Bell in Philadelphia?

2. Which sentence expresses the ideal attitude to one's neighbor?

3. The Torah uses a cycle of years for conducting social and business affairs. What is the seventh year called? And the fiftieth year?

4. What are the agricultural laws designed to help the poor?

5. What is the reference to the Lulav and Etrog used on Sukkot in the Torah?

6. What musical instrument was used in Biblical times to proclaim the Jubilee year?

7. In connection with what are the following phrases used in Leviticus?
a. The forth year.      b. The fifth year.      c. The sixth year.

8. The Jubilee year generally brought a return of sold property to the original ownership, thus ensuring the maintenance or equitable land distribution in Israel. However:
a. What type of property did not go out in the Jubilee year?
b. What type of property had a "perpetual" right to redemption?
c. What type of property could not even be sold?

9. Why were the Children of Israel not allowed to sell land in perpetuity, besides the reason of equitable land distribution?

10. On which day and in which Hebrew month named in the Torah do the following holidays fall:
a. Passover          b. Rosh Hashanah
c. Yom Kippur        d. Sukkot

11. Give the sentence in Leviticus which pertains to honest weights and measures?

12. In the portion of Mishpatim, it says, "If you buy a Hebrew servant." Give an example of a situation which can cause an Israelite to become a slave.

13. Iron and copper are mentioned in the Torah by Moses in speaking of the Land of Israel. Where are they mentioned as a dire prediction and in what connection?

14. Give two examples of passages from Leviticus from which we learn about the equality of all inhabitants in the Land of Israel in a court of law.

15. To whom is the following reference made? "Love him as yourself; for you were…in the land of Egypt."

16. List the "four species" that we use on Sukkot and give their Biblical description.

17. What is the rule about payment to a hired servant?

18. The Urim and the Tumim were special items worn by whom?

19. What happened to two sons of Aaron?

20. A male Jewish child is to be circumcised on which day that follows his birth?

21. Which group of the Children of Israel had the role of what we might call today a "health officer?"

22. What does the Torah say is the principal carrier of life in an animal?

23. What does the Book of Leviticus say in reference to Child-Parent relations?

24. How are we to treat the elderly, according to Leviticus?

25. What does the Torah say about "gossip?"

26. What are the regulations about a Kohen, regarding contact with the dead?

ר

ר

ק

ר

א

27. What are the regulations regarding the High Priest's (Kohen Gadol) contact with the dead?

28. What was the law and penalty in Biblical times for blasphemy?

29. The numbers "5", "100", and "10,000" are used in one sentence. Are these numbers a blessing (reward) or a curse (punishment)?

30. Identify: a. Molech; b. Azazel

31. Identify: a. Seven weeks; b. Seven years; c. Seven times seven.

32. How are we supposed to treat people who are deaf and / or blind?

33. If we see a neighbor doing something wrong, what are we supposed to do?

34. What other name for Yom Kippur is given in Leviticus?

35. Who is forbidden to drink wine or other strong drinks when they go into the "Tent of Meeting?"

36. What punishment is to be meted out to a person who curses his parents?

37. Why were the seven nations of Canaan ordered by God to be destroyed?

38. What custom, that was practiced to anoint the High Priest, is practiced until this day by the British Royal Family?

39. Were there any men of the Priestly family that were forbidden to serve in the Tabernacle or later in the Temple?

40. Who's duty was it to attend to the lighting of the Menorah in the Sanctuary?

# Quiz Me On The Book Of Numbers

Sources and answers to this section begin on page 142

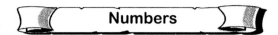

**Numbers**

# Multiple Choice Questions

1. From the case of the daughters of Zelophechad, we were to learn the laws relating to:
a. Widows and orphans
b. Marriage and divorce
c. Inheritance
d. Honoring one's parents

2. When were farmers obliged to "Bring an offering of newly harvested grains"?
a. During the festival of Passover
b. On the day of the first fruits (Shavuot)
c. On the first day of Nissan
d. During the festival of Sukkot

3. The statement "To the more you shall give the more inheritance, and to the fewer you shall give the less inheritance" refers to:
a. The gifts given to the priests
b. The daily gathering of the manna
c. The division of the land of Israel among the tribes
d. The land allocated to Reuben and Gad across the Jordan River

4. "Take more from the larger groups and less from the smaller" refers to:
a. The cities of refuge
b. The sacrificial offerings
c. The spoils distributed from Midian
d. The division of the land of Israel among the tribes

5. The request "They marry into a clan of their father's tribe" underscores that:
a. Only the father voids a marriage vow of an unmarried daughter
b. Women were not to be given inheritance in the Land of Israel
c. Inheritances of the Israelites shall not be removed from tribe to tribe
d. An orphan daughter is duty bound to perpetuate the name of her father

6. The term "Until the death of the High Priest" applies to:
a. The laws of defilement of the dead      b. The replacement of Aaron by Elazar
c. The laws of the Nazarite      d. The laws of manslaughter

7. The sprouting of Aaron's staff proved that:
a. Even a dry rod could blossom in an environment of sanctity
b. It was God who appointed Aaron to the High Priesthood
c. Aaron, like Moses, had the privilege of using the sacred staff
d. Aaron alone possessed the power of working plagues

8. The verse recited in the beginning of the morning prayers contains the phrase "How goodly are thy tents, O Jacob, thy dwellings, O Israel!" is taken from:
a. The prayers of Moses      b. The song of the well
c. The blessings of Balaam      d. The book of wars of the Lord

9. "And grant you peace" is the conclusion of:
a. Moses' agreement with Reuben and Gad
b. The priestly benediction
c. Balak's message to Balaam
d. Moses' message to the King of Edom

10. The place "Kibroth-hattaavah" is associated with the sin of:
a. The craving for eating meat
b. The spies because of their report
c. The Israelite's transgression with the daughter of Moab
d. The waters of Meribah

11. The Amalekites and the Canaanites succeeded in smiting the Israelites at Hormah because:
a. They outnumbered the Israelites
b. They used the technique of surprise attack
c. Joshua did not lead the army into battle
d. The Israelites went to war without Moses' permission

12. The laws relating to purging of the vessels are taught in connection with:
a. The war of Midian      b. The sending of spies
c. The strife with Korach      d. The war with Sihon and Og

13. Under certain circumstances, which holiday may be celebrated a month late?
a. Shavuot                          b. Passover
c. Sukkot                           d. Rosh Hashanah

14. Which land (other than Israel) is referred to as:
"A land flowing with milk and honey"?
a. The land of Egypt                b. The land of Midian
c. The land of Moab                 d. The land of Edom

15. Whose place did the Levites take in the service of God?
a. The Priests'                     b. The young prophets'
c. Those drafted into the army      d. The first-born of the Children of Israel

16. What kind of fruit did the spies bring back from the Land of Canaan?
a. Figs, pomegranates and bokser
b. Pomegranates, nuts and bokser
c. A cluster of grapes, pomegranates, and figs
d. A cluster of grapes, bokser, and pomegranates

17. To which place did Balak take Balaam to curse the Children of Israel?
a. Hor Hahar                        b. Kiriath-Chutzoth
c. Bamot Baal                       d. Mount Nebo

18. In which war did even the Levites participate?
a. The war with Midian              b. The war with Amalek
c. The war with Sihon and Og        d. The war with Ai

19. How are vessels that are used on fire made kosher?
a. By dipping them into hot water   b. By dipping them into lukewarm water
c. By passing them into fire        d. By burying them for three days

20. What did Moses suggest to the sons of Gad and Reuben be built on the east side of Jordan?
a. Schools                          b. Synagogues
c. A holy temple                    d. Sheepfolds for their cattle and cities for their families

במדבר

21. How does the Torah describe Moses' character?
a. He was wiser than all men
b. He was very humble above all the men that were on the face of the earth
c. He was a man of integrity
d. He was a generous person

22. What prayer did Moses offer in behalf of his sister Miriam?
a. Heal us, O Lord, and we shall be healed
b. Please, O Lord, send her a complete recovery
c. Merciful Healer, grant complete healing
d. Heal her now, O God, I beseech thee

23. Why were Moses and Aaron not privileged to enter the Land of Canaan?
a. Because they were among the spies
b. Because they rebelled against God at the waters of Meribah
c. Because the people demanded that Joshua should lead them into the land
d. Because they refused to fight for the land

24. What did Moses ask God to do for the Children of Israel before he died?
a. That he appoint a leader over the people to replace him
b. That his brother Aaron become the next leader
c. That Caleb, the son of Jephuneh become the leader
d. That he forgive them for the sin of the Golden Calf

25. Under what condition did Moses agree to give the sons of Reuben, Gad and half the tribe of Menashe their inheritance on the east side of Jordan?
a. That they themselves will conquer the east side of the Jordan
b. That they will be the vanguard of the army until they subdue the enemy
c. That they will keep their reserve units in the Land of Canaan when needed
d. That their daughters will marry men from the other 9-1/2 tribes

26. Why was Miriam punished?
a. Because she refused to cross the Jordan
b. Because she demanded equal rights with men
c. Because she wanted to be the leader of the people
d. Because she spoke against Moses

במדבר

27. What were the duties of the Levites with respect to the Tabernacle?
a. To sacrifice the offerings of the Israelites
b. To help Moses teach the Torah
c. To carry the Tabernacle and its vessels and to guard them
d. To help Moses judge the people

28. How many cities were given to the Levites?
a. Twenty            b. Thirty
c. Forty-eight       d. One hundred and twenty

29. In what connection was the expression "Are the people who dwell in it (Canaan) strong or weak" used?
a. The prophecy of Balaam
b. Moses' prayer for Miriam
c. Part of the instructions given to the spies
d. The prayer of Hannah

30. Who directed the Children of Israel during their journey in the desert?
a. Aaron       b. God       c. Judah       d. Joshua

31. The statement: "Since theirs was the service of the (most) sacred objects, their porterage was by shoulder" suggests that:
a. The priests must wear their sacred garments on their shoulders
b. Every sacred object is to be carried on the shoulders
c. Only those who carry sacred objects upon their shoulders qualify for priestly consideration
d. The Holy Ark may not be carried on wagons

32. The punishment "A fire of the Lord broke out against them" came for the sin of:
a. "Who shall give us flesh to eat"
b. "Let Us make a captain and let us return to Egypt"
c. "The people took to complaining bitterly before the Lord"
d. "You have killed the people of the Lord"

68

33. "The water of bitterness" is mentioned in connection with
a. Israel's complaints against Moses
b. The cleansing process from defilement by the dead.
c. A man's wife who goes astray
d. The death of Miriam.

34. Where is Agag's name mentioned in the Torah?
a. In the list of Israel's journeys in the desert
b. In the wars with Sihon and Og
c. In Balaam's blessings
d. In the conditions of Reuben and Gad

35. The value of "The five shekels by the sanctuary weight which is twenty gerahs" appears in reference to the commandment of?
a. The return of stolen property
b. The offering of the paschal sacrifice
c. The heave offering
d. The redemption of the first-born

36. Who was the one that was "placed in custody"?
a. The man gathering sticks          b. The manslayer
c. The avenger                       d. Miriam

37. The phrase "food due me" refers to
a. Manna          b. Show bread
c. Quail          d. Daily offerings

38. Which object of jewels does not belong in the listed group
a. Chains          b. Bracelets
c. Rings           d. Nose rings

39. One of the tribes that did not camp on the eastern side was
a. Judah           b. Reuben
c. Issaschar       d. Zebulun

במדבר

40. The request "they marry into a clan of their father's tribe" underscores that:
a. Only a father voids a vow of an unmarried daughter
b. Women are not to be given inheritance in the Land of Israel
c. Inheritance of the Children of Israel shall not remove from tribe to tribe
d. That an orphan daughter is duty bound to perpetuate the name of her father

41. The Levites were eligible to serve in the Tabernacle from the age of:
a. One month and up
b. Twenty years and over
c. From thirteen years and up
d. From thirty years to fifty years

42. Which of the following is given to the Levites
a. First fruit
b. Heave offering
c. Tithes
d. First-born

43. "One tenth of the tithe" is given
a. By the Israelites to the priest
b. By the priest to the Levite
c. By the Levites to the priest
d. By the Israelites to the Levite

44. The one that was not required to be put out of the camp was:
a. The Leper
b. Anyone with an eruption or discharge
c. A man's wife who goes astray
d. Whoever is defiled by the dead

45. "Cedar wood, hyssop and scarlet" bring to mind:
a. The paschal sacrifice
b. The staff of Aaron
c. Red heifer
d. The priestly garments

46. The plating for the altar serves a reminder that:
a. It is not permissible to offer strange fire upon the altar
b. No stranger may offer incense before the Lord
c. A golden censer is an unfit vessel for incense offering
d. The altar must be covered when carried from place to place

47. Who became the high priest after the death of Aaron?
a. Pinchas    b. Itamar    c. Elazar    d. Nadav

48. To which King did Moses ask permission to pass through his land?
a. King of Edom　　　　b. King of Midian
c. King of Moab　　　　d. King of Ammon

49. The flag of which camp was in the rear of all the camps in the wilderness?
a. Reuben　　　　b. Judah
c. Dan　　　　d. Ephraim

50. Who has the power to disallow the vow of a woman whose husband died?
a. Her father　　　　b. The Priest
c. The tribal head　　　　d. No one

51. When is a manslayer who killed unintentionally, permitted to leave the city of refuge?
a. Upon the death of the king
b. Upon the death of the high priest
c. Upon the death of the avenger of blood
d. After six years

52. In connection with what event did Moses and Aaron say, "Hear now ye rebels"?
a. The rebellion of Korach　　　　b. The spies
c. The waters of Meribah　　　　d. The lusting for meat

53. What reward did Pinchas receive for "turning away God's wrath from the Children of Israel"?
a. He became High Priest after Aaron
b. He was chosen leader after the death of Moses
c. He was granted a covenant for an everlasting priesthood
d. He became a Prophet.

54. The standard of which camp was the first to move forward in the journeys of the Children of Israel in the wilderness of Sinai?
a. Camp of Reuben　　　　b. Camp of Judah
c. Camp of Ephraim　　　　d. Camp of Dan

במדבר

55. All those who were able to go forth to war were numbered in the wilderness. From what age and upward were they counted?
a. Eighteen          b. Twenty
c. Twenty-five       d. Thirty

56. "We have sinned because we have spoken against the Lord and against thee." These words were said by the Children of Israel after what incident?
a. Korach's rebellion
b. Fiery serpents
c. The spies
d. The waters of Meribah

57. Aaron, the High Priest, died in the wilderness and did not deserve to see the Promised Land because of what sin?
a. He spoke evil of Moses
b. He helped the multitude to make the Golden Calf
c. He did riot restrain his sons from offering strange fire
d. He rebelled against the Lord's word at the waters of Meribah

58. According to the Torah, if a man left no son and no daughter, who was next in line to receive his inheritance?
a. His father's brothers    b. His brothers
c. His father's father       d. His father's sisters

59. Upon whom did the Lord bestow His spirit so that they should bear the burden of the people together with Moses?
a. The Levites
b. Aaron and his sons
c. The princes of the tribes
d. The seventy Elders

60. "Shall one man sin, and wilt thou be wroth with all the congregation?" These words were said in connection with what event?
a. Report of the spies       b. Rebellion of Korach
c. Waters of Meribah         d. Craving for meat

61. If a man killed a person unintentionally, he could save his life by:
a. Paying a ransom to the family of the deceased
b. Bringing a sacrifice to the Priest
c. Fleeing to the city of refuge
d. Taking hold of the corners of the altar

62. "And behold ye are risen up in your father's stead, a brood of sinful men." To whom did Moses address these sharp words?
a. Korach and his congregation      b. Tribes of Gad and Reuben
c. The spies      d. The multitude that lusted for meat

63. The daughters of Zelophechad stated that their father died in the wilderness because of his sin. What was his sin?
a. He participated in the rebellion of Korach    b. He worshiped the Golden Calf
c. He was among those who craved meat      d. His sin is not told in the Torah

64. What object placed before the Testimony in the Tabernacle was kept against the rebellious children?
a. Rod of Aaron      b. Rod of Moses      c. Bronze snake      d. Jar of manna

65. Why did the tribes of Gad and Reuben request that the land east of the Jordan be given to them as their possession?
a. Because they wanted to be the first tribes to receive their inheritance
b. Because the land was fertile and they had lots of cattle
c. Because they had no desire to cross the Jordan and fight the nations of Canaan
d. Because they thought they would receive a smaller possession in Canaan

66. Why did the Lord send fiery serpents among the people?
a. Because they believed the words of the spies
b. Because they wanted to stone Joshua and Caleb
c. Because they said "Let us appoint a leader and return to Egypt"
d. Because they complained about the manna and the lack of bread and water

67. "And they put Me to proof (test) ten times in the wilderness" was said in connection with:
a. The reports of the spies      b. The rebellion of Korach
c. The complaints about the manna      d. The waters of Meribah

במדבר

68. Why was the command "Only into the family of the tribe of their father shall they be married" said?
a. Because the father may disallow his daughter's vows
b. So that the husband should not be jealous of his wife
c. So that no inheritance shall be moved from tribe to tribe
d. Because women had no share in the Land of Israel

69. What did the Children of Israel and the "mixed multitude" lust for?
a. The drinking of water
b. The eating of meat
c. The going to war
d. The assuming of leadership

70. What does the name Kibroth-hattaavah suggest to us?
a. The quail
b. The sin of the spies
c. The waters of strife
d. The sin with the daughters of Midian

71. When is a new meal-offering brought to God?
a. On the day of Shavuot                b. During the festival of Passover
c. On the first day of Nissan           d. During the festival of Sukkot

72. What was the age span of the Levites in the service of God?
a. 25-45          b. 25-50
c. 13-70          d. 18-65

73. The law of the Nazarite does not include which of the following?
a. Abstinence from liquor      b. Abstinence from wine
c. Fasting                     d. Allowing the hair to grow

74. For which one of the following reasons must a Jewish person delay his observance of Passover for one month?
a. He didn't have his matzos baked in time
b. He was unclean by reason of a dead body
c. He was unclean by reason of unclean food
d. He became involved in Tzedekah work

75. In the desert, by what means did Moses signal the Children of Israel to congregate or travel?
a. By shouting orders
b. By blowing two "shofarot"
c. By waving flags
d. By blowing two silver trumpets

76. What was the reaction of the Children of Israel to the report given by the group of ten spies who returned from Canaan?
a. Go quickly to the Promised Land
b. Make a captain and return to Egypt
c. Build altars and offer sacrifices
d. Give these men a special reward

77. Who from among the people of the generation of the spies would God allow to enter the Land of Israel?
a. The little ones
b. The righteous ones
c. The spies
d. The seventy Elders

# About Whom Or What Is It Said?

1. "Are you wrought up on my account?"

2. "By displaying among them his passion for me"

3. "And in color it was like bdellium"

4. "Do not fear him for I give him and all his people and his land unto your hand"

5. "He was not one of the faction ... Who banded together against the Lord"

6. "And lay your hand upon him"

7. "Is the Lord's Hand waxed short?"

8. "He is trusted in all my house"

9. "Behold, I come forth for an adversary, because your way is contrary to me"

10. And ground it in mills, or beat it in mortars, and seethed it in pots"

במדבר

11. And they "Departed with the rewards of divination in their hand"

12. "And they bore it upon a pole between two"

13. "And put forth buds, and bloomed blossoms, and bore ripe almonds"

14. "He shall dwell therein until the death of the high priest"

15. "Have received their inheritance beyond the Jordan at Jericho, eastward toward the rising sun"

16. "He went not, as at other times"

17. "And they returned...at the end of forty days"

18. "Look at it and recall all the commandments of the Lord"

19. "And the spirit of jealousy came upon him"

20. "You shall set it aside as a gift like the gift from the threshing floor"

21. "...in which there is no defect and on which no yoke has been laid"

22. "With his sword drawn in his hand"

23. "At his word they shall go out and at his word they shall come in"

24. "He smote (clapped) his hands together"

25. "They shall leave none of it unto the morning"

26. "He hath another spirit and hath followed me"

27. "A man in whom there is spirit.

28. "No razor shall come upon his head"

29. "Set it upon a pole"

ב

מ

ד

ב

ר

30. "(It) bore ripe almonds"

31. "For they are wholly given unto me"

32. "We were in our own sight as grasshoppers"

33. "That these men have despised the Lord"

# Who Are They?

1. The sister that spoke out against her brother.

2. The disciple whose teacher added one letter to his name.

3. The leader of a tribe who was killed by a zealot.

4. The father who left only daughters behind him.

5. The son who wore his father's garments.

6. The one who may not be defiled even by his own dead father or mother.

7. The tribe that was not counted among the other tribes.

8.  He warred against Israel and took many captives.

9. "And took a spear in his hand"

10. "He went not as other times to meet with enchantments"

11. They showed the Children of Israel the fruits of Israel.

12. He didn't allow the Children of Israel to cross his border

13. "And they had no children"

במדבר

# Who Said To Whom?

1. "Lay not, I pray thee, sin upon us , for that we have done foolishly and for that we have sinned"

2. "Come thou with us, and we will do thee good"

3. "With him do I speak mouth to mouth, even manifestly"

4. "It is a land that eateth up the inhabitants thereof"

5. "Thou shall not pass through me, lest I come out with the sword against thee"

6. "The land, which we passed through is an exceeding good land"

7. "Am I not able indeed to promote thee to honor?"

8. "I have not taken one ass from them, neither have I hurt one of them"

9. "Ye take too much upon you, seeing all the congregation are holy ...and the Lord is among them; wherefore then lift up yourselves above the assembly of the Lord?"

10. "Your servants will do as my Lord commands"

11. "Is there a limit to the Lord's power?"

12. "Have I been in the habit of doing this to you?"

13. "May the Lord make you a curse and an imprecation"

14. "Avenge the Children of Israel"

15. "Am I really unable to reward you?

16. "Was I ever want to do so unto thee?"

17. "Then ye shall be cleared before the Lord and before Israel"

18. "I will depart to mine own land and to my kindred"

19. "And thou shalt be to us instead of eyes"

20. "If I had a sword in my hand, for now I had killed thee"

21. "What men are these with thee"

22. "Behold I give unto him my covenant of peace"

23. "Behold they cover the face of the earth"

24. "Shall your brethren go to war and shall ye sit here?"

25. "I wish that all the Lord's people were prophets"

26. "Thou knowest all the travail that hath befallen us"

27. "Let us make a captain, and let us return into Egypt"

28. "We remember the fish which we used to eat free in Egypt"

29. "Have I conceived all this people"

30. "We should go up at once and possess it"

# Unique Questions

1. From which country are the following?
a. Hobab          b. King of Arad          c. Sichon

2. Name the two people referred by God as "My servant".

3. Two people stopped a plague. Who were they and how did they do it?

4. Whom or what were the following said to be like?

a. Grasshoppers                    b. Snow

c. Coriander seed                  d. A lioness

5. Which incidents in the Book of Numbers endured the following amount of time?

a. Seven days          b. Forty days          c. A month

6. What were the three expressions the spies used in their report about the Land.

7. Name three kings who waged war against the Children of Israel, two physically and one with words.

8. Opposing the report of the ten spies about the evils of the Land were the remaining two spies. Quote two expressions of what they said.

9. From which place did Moses see the Land of Israel? From which place did Balaam see the Children of Israel?

10. From the words of Balaam, give two verses that reveal the uniqueness of the nation of Israel.

11. Name six metals found in one verse in the Book of Numbers

12. What are the five ornaments worn by women that are mentioned in one verse in the Book of Numbers?

13. Name three things prohibited for the Nazarite.

14. Name three things the spies were to investigate in the land of Canaan.

15. What were the complaints of Korach and his followers against Moses and Aaron?

16. Moses had to ask God for instructions regarding three important matters. What were they?

17. With what event are Almonds and Figs associated?

במדבר

18. Which two sons of Aaron were punished for bringing strange fire into the Tabernacle?

19. About whom did Joshua say to Moses, "My Lord Moses shut, them in" and what was Moses' reply?

20. Moses sent messengers to two kings asking for permission to pass through their land? Who were the kings?

21. Who was Moses' successor? And how was the act of appointment accomplished?

# Match The Verses

1. "It is a people that shall dwell alone"

2. "Let me die the death of the righteous"

3. "There shall step forth a star out of Jacob"

4. "And his king shall be higher than Agag"

5. "God who brought him forth out of Egypt"

6. "God is not a man, that He should lie"

7. "Who hath counted the dust of Jacob"

8. "For there is no enchantment with Jacob"

9. "I see him but not now"

10. "Water shall flow from his branches"

11. "Amalek was the first of the nations"

במדבר

# Fill In The Missing Words

1. Lo, it is a people that dwelleth …. and is not …. among the nations.

2. Shall your brethren go to …. and shall ye sit ….

3. Shall one man …. and wilt thou be wroth with all the congregation.

4. The Lord lifts up his …. upon thee and give thee ….

5. Rise up, Lord, and let thine …. be scattered, and let them that hate thee flee before thee.

6. And let …. before the Lord, and before Israel.

7. That the congregation of the Lord be not as …. which have no …..

8. The well which the …. dug, which the …. of the people delved

9. And our …. loatheth this light ….

10. The Lord make His …. to shine upon thee and be …. unto thee.

11. Moses was very …. above all the men that were on the ….
of the earth.

12. I wish that all the Lord's …. were ….

13. Pardon, I pray Thee, the …. of this people according unto the …. of thy loving kindness.

14. That they put with the …. of each corner a thread of ….

15. Ye shall have one statute both for the …. and for him that is …. in the land.

16. Rise up O Lord and let thine …. be ….

17. The Lord is slow to …. and plenteous in ….

18. Behold a people that rises up like a …. and as a …. does he lift himself up.

19. So shall they put my …. upon the Children of Israel, and I will …. them.

20. You shall blow with the …. over your burnt offerings and over the sacrifices of your ….

21. Of the first of your … you shall give unto the Lord a portion for a … throughout your generations.

22. The Lord …. thee and …. thee.

23. How goodly are thy …., O Jacob, Thy …. O Israel.

# Identify The Relationship

1. Serach to Asher

2. Jochebed to Amram

3. Pinchas to Aaron

4. Hobab to Moses

5. Uziel to Aaron

6. Itamar to Elazar

7. Amminadav to Nahshon

8. Mahlah to Tirzah

9. Eliav to Dathan

10. Jochebed to Miriam

11. Nun to Joshua

12. Dathan to Eliav

# Match The Place With The Event

1. Shittim

2. Hatzerot

3. Desert of Zin

4. Kibroth-hattaavah

5. Mount Hor

6. Mount Avarim (Nebo)

במדבר

7. Elim

8. Rameses

# Identify The Names From The Descriptions

1. "The man whose eyes are open"

2. The Ethiopian woman

3. The servant of Moses

4. The people of Chemosh

5. The men of great stature

6. The daughter of a prince of Midian who allured a prince of Israel

7. Fought against Israel and took some of them prisoner

8. The woman who responds: "Amen, amen"

9. Meek above all the men

10. The minister of Moses

# Identify The Son

1. The son of Beor

2. The son of Amram

3. The son of Nun

4. The son of Jephuneh

# Quiz Me On The Book Of Deuteronomy

Sources and answers to this section begin on page 156

# Multiple Choice Questions

1. According to the Torah, how long is a man supposed to cheer his new wife?
a. One week
b. One month
c. Three months
d. One year

2. To whom did Moses send messengers with words of peace?
a. Sihon, king of Heshbon
b. The king of Moab
c. Og, king of Bashan
d. The king of Midian

3. Which sin is inferred by the expression "Entice thee secretly"?
a. To intermarry with the surrounding nations
b. To go and serve other gods
c. To leave the land of Israel
d. Not to observe the Sabbath

4. Who is the false one referred to by the verse, "Then shall ye do unto him as he had purposed to do unto his brother"?
a. The murderer
b. The thief
c. The witness
d. The Judge

5. What is the intention of the verse, "Thou shalt not harden thy heart nor shut thy hand from thy…. brother"?
a. To the mitzvah of charity
b. To the priestly gifts
c. To the wages of the hired hand
d. To the second tithe

6. What is a king of Israel forbidden to increase among his possessions?
a. Soldiers                    b. Women and horses
c. Slaves and handmaidens    d. Ministers

7. When do the Elders of a city bring a heifer "Which has not drawn in the yoke"?
a. Over the war dead             b. Over the dead of the courts
c. Over one found slain in the field    d. Over the death of the high-priest

8. In the Torah it says, "Thou shalt not wear a mingled stuff." What materials are referred to?
a. Silk and linen              b. Wool and silk
c. Wool and linen            d. Sackcloth and silk

9. What did Moses command the Children of Israel to set up immediately after they would pass over the Jordan?
a. A sanctuary               b. The Israelitish camp
c. Great stones              d. The great Temple

10. About which tribe was the following blessing said: "Let him be the favored of his brethren, and let him dip his foot in oil"?
a. Asher       b. Judah
c. Joseph     d. Dan

11. How can a person who has killed someone involuntarily save his own life?
a. By holding onto the corners of the altar    b. By offering a sacrifice
c. By fleeing to a city of refuge          d. By confessing to the Priest

12. What did the Torah command to do "from the time the sickle is first put to the standing corn"?
a. To observe the holiday of Passover
b. To observe the holiday of Weeks (Shavuot)
c. To observe the holiday of Sukkot
d. To count seven weeks

13. In which generation would an Egyptian be permitted to enter into the assembly of the Lord?
a. The seventh generation      b. The third generation
c. Never                  d. The tenth generation

14. In which land did Moses explain the law (Torah) to the Children of Israel?
a. Israel                    b. Egypt
c. Moab                    d. Edom

15. Why did God choose Israel as His own treasure?
a. Because the Children of Israel where the most numerous of all the nations
b. Because God loved them
c. Because the other nations did not want this honor
d. Because the Children of Israel asked this of God

16. Why were the Children of Israel commanded to love the stranger?
a. Because they were strangers in the Land of Egypt
b. Because they hated strangers
c. Because the strangers fought against Israel
d. Because the strangers served the Children of Israel

17. What is done to the Hebrew slave who refuses to leave his master?
a. He is sent to freedom
b. An awl is thrust through his ear
c. He is given more severance pay
d. He is not heard at all

18. Why did not God permit the Children of Israel to wage war with Moab and Seir?
a. Because they were too strong
b. Because the Children of Israel sinned by sending spies to Canaan
c. Because God gave them their lands as an inheritance
d. Because the Children of Israel had no army at that time

19. About which land is it written, "And thou didst water it with thy foot, as a garden of herbs"?
a. Egypt                    b. Canaan
c. The Negev                d. Jordan

20. Who were the ones who declared: "Our hands have not shed this blood"?
a. The Judges                b. The Elders
c. The Priests                d. The Levites

21. When is the following phrase recited, "A wandering Aramean was my father, and he went down to Egypt"?
a. At the bringing of the Omer
b. At the bringing of the first-fruits
c. During the year of Shmitah
d. On the holiday of the ingathering

22. Which unclean animal chews its cud but does not have cloven hoofs?
a. A sheep
b. A cow
c. A pig
d. A camel

23. Who speaks to the Jewish soldiers before they go out to war?
a. The Priest
b. The Levite
c. The King
d. The tribal head

24. What is to be tied to the four corners of a garment?
a. A rope
b. A belt
c. Twisted strings
d. A pair of pants

25. About whom is it written, "His eye was not dim nor his natural force abated"?
a. Elazar
b. Joshua
c. Aaron
d. Moses

26. Whose curses did God turn into blessings?
a. Korach
b. Balak
c. Balaam
d. Zimri

27. In which connection is the following said, "Thou mayest not hide thyself"?
a. A vow
b. A lost thing
c. Charity
d. A blind person

28. To whom should the first fruits be brought?
a. To the strangers
b. To the elders
c. To the poor
d. To the Kohen

29. To what age did Moses live?
a. 70 years
b. 120 years
c. 149 years
d. 77 years

30. If you employ a day-laborer, when, according to the Torah, are you required to pay him his wages?
a. At the end of the week       b. At the new moon
c. The same day                       d. When the job is finished

31. Who spoke the song which begins with the following words: "Give ear ye heavens and I will speak and let the earth hear the words of my mouth"
a. Miriam       b. Aaron       c. Deborah       d. Moses

32. Who is referred to in the following Biblical passage? "Encourage him and strengthen him for he shall go over before this people."
a. Aaron       b. Moses       c. Joshua       d. Caleb

33. To whom did Moses send the following message? "Let me pass through thy land, …thou shalt sell me food for money that I may eat and give me water for money that I may drink."
a. Og, King of Bashan
b. Debir, King of Eglon
c. Sihon, King of Heshbon
d. Piram, King of Yarmuth

34. According to the Torah, how many witnesses are required in order to establish that a man has sinned?
a. Two or three           b. One is sufficient
c. Four                         d. Six

35. "When thou shall besiege a city a long time in making war against it," what trees does the Torah command us to leave uncut?
a. Newly flanked trees
b. Those that are for food
c. Evergreen trees
d. Cedar trees

36. Which Canaanite king had a bedstead of iron nine cubits in length and four cubits in breadth?
a. Og, King of Bashan
b. Yavin, King of Hazor
c. Sihon, King of Heshbon
d. Japhia, King of Lachish

37. Which of the following does not belong in this group?
a. Altars     b. Pillars     c. Leafy trees          d. Fruit trees

38. "At the end of every .... years, even in the same year, you shall bring forth all the tithe of your increase."  What is the missing number?
a. Two          b. Three       c. Four       d. Five

39. "Remember what the Lord your God did unto Miriam" refers to:
a. The Red Sea          b. The Golden Calf
c. Leprosy                 d. The well

40. The wish of Israel to be "like all the nations that are round about me" refers to the choosing of:
a. General      b. King        c. Judge      d. High priest

41. "...and you shall not eat the life with the flesh" refers to:
a. The sinews  b. The veins    c. The heart    d. The blood

42. "...of their flesh you shall not eat" refers to all of the following except:
a. Camel        b. Ox          c. Hare       d. Rock-badger

43. How many portions of his father's inheritance does the first-born son receive?
a. Double portion               b. The entire amount
c. The same as the other sons     d. Triple the others

44. How long did the Children of Israel mourn after the death of Moses?
a. An entire year   b. Seven months   c. Thirty days   d. Seven weeks

45. According to the Book of Deuteronomy, what was the name of the Hebrew month in which Passover was celebrated?
a. Nissan       b. Shvat   c. Tammuz  d. Aviv

46.  Which holiday is associated with the threshing-floor and the wine press?
a. Passover    b. Sukkot              c. Feast of Weeks      d. Feast of Matzot

47. By what other name is Mount Sinai known?
a. Carmel       b. Tabor              c. Pisgah                d. Horeb

דברים

48. By what other name is the Salt Sea (Dead Sea) known in Deuteronomy?
a. The Sea of the Arabah      b. Sea of Galilee
c. Sea of Reeds                d. Black Sea

49. Moses appointed captains of thousands, hundreds, fifties and tens to assist him. What qualities did he look for in these leaders?
a. Strong men                b. Men of courage
c. Good family background    d. Wise men, full of knowledge

50. How many Israelite tribes settled east of the Jordan River?
a. One          b. None          c. Two and a half      d. Four

51. Moses was not permitted to enter the Promised Land but he was able to see it from a mountain top. What was the name of this mountain?
a. Gerizim      b. Sinai              c. Nebo                d. Ebal

52. Under whose leadership did the Israelites enter the Promised Land?
a. Moses        b. Aaron              c. Caleb              d. Joshua

53. How many cities of refuge did Moses establish east of the Jordan River?
a. Three        b. Seven              c. Thirteen          d. Ten

54. In Chapter 6 of Deuteronomy it is written: "And you shall write them upon the doorposts of your house, and upon your gates." To what ritual object does this refer?
a. Yad          b. Mezuzah            c. Mizrach            d. Menorah

55. How long did Moses stay on Mount Sinai?
a. An entire month
b. A week and a day
c. Forty days
d. Seven weeks

56. How did Moses react when he saw the Israelites worshipping the Golden Calf?
a. He threw down the tablets and broke them
b. He fasted for an entire week
c. He wept in despair
d. He put on sackcloth and ashes

57. According to Deuteronomy, what did the Canaanites do "upon the mountains, and upon the hills, and under every leafy tree?"
a. They greeted the new moon          b. They worshipped their idols
c. They held a council of war          d. They conducted weddings

58. One of the following may not share in the tithe:
a. Fatherless     b. Levite        c. Prophet          d. Stranger

59. Of the following, which one is not a pilgrimage festival?
a. Passover     b. Shavuot      c. Rosh Hashanah      d. Sukkot

60. What punishment does the Torah require for a false witness?
a. He receives the same punishment that he sought to inflict
b. He must pay a fine of twenty shekels of silver
c. He is sentenced to one year in prison
d. He must spend six months in servitude

61. If a poor man gives his garment as a pledge, when must the lender return it?
a. When the sun goes down
b. When the money is paid back
c. No later than one month
d. Before the next Sabbath

62. The tribe that stood neither on Grizim nor Ebal was:
a. Simeon       b. Judah        c. Dan              d. Menashe

63. "Let me not hear the voice of the Lord my God" was said in:
a. Egypt        b. Horeb        c. Kadesh Barnea      d. Mount Nebo

64. "Iron and brass shall be your bars" refers to the tribe of:
a. Judah        b. Reuben       c. Zebulun          d. Asher

65. Which nation chased the Israelites "as bees do, and beat you down in Seir"?
a. Edom         b. Amalek       c. Amorites         d. Ammon

66. So "that innocent blood be not shed in the midst of the land" God commanded the Israelites to choose special:
a. Courts       b. Judges       c. Cities           d. Princes

67. "That you bring not blood guilt upon your house" refers to the building of a:
a. Bulwark      b. Gate      c. Wall      d. Parapet

68. The Torah teaches you shall not hate an Edomite because?
a. You were a stranger in his land
b. He is your brother
c. He allowed the Israelites to pass through his country
d. He helped the Israelites to fight their enemies

69. If an unmarried brother of a deceased does not wish to marry his widowed sister-in-law, what does the sister-in-law remove from her brother-in-law?
a. His ring      b. His hat      c. His sandal      d. His tallit

70. In the Book of Deuteronomy we find another expression for the word "matzah." It is called bread of:
a. Redemption      b. Poverty
c. Slavery      d. Freedom

71. The Land of Israel was blessed with seven kinds of choice products. Which of the following is not mentioned among them?
a. Wheat      b. Barley      c. Wines      d. Nuts

72. The mountain which is called Sion, Senir and Sirion is also known as?
a. Nebo      b. Hermon      c. Horeb      d. Seir

73. Which of the following is not included in the restriction which the Torah states "You shall not eat of their flesh?"
a. Gazelle      b. Camel      c. Rabbit      d. Hare

74. Who of the following is not exempt from going to war?
a. Anyone who has not dedicated his newly built house
b. Anyone who has a small child
c. Anyone who has not harvested his newly planted vineyard
d. Anyone who is afraid

75. Who died on Hor Ha-har?
a. Aaron      b. Moses
c. Miriam      d. Zelophechad

76. During the 40 years in the wilderness, the Israelites did not have to replace their?

a. Pots          b. Tents          c. Shoes          d. Blankets

# About Whom Or What Was It Said?

1. "Thy Tummim and Thy Urim be with the holy one."

2. "A lion's whelp, that leapeth forth from Bashan."

3. "That he shall write him a copy of this law in a book."

4. "Thou shalt bring it home and it shall be with thee until thy brother require it."

5. "Because they met you not with bread and water."

6. "I have put away the hollowed things out of my house."

7. "It is not in heaven."

8. "Thou shalt furnish him liberally out of thy flock."

9. "He surprised you on the march, when you were famished and weary, and cut down all the stragglers in your rear."

10. "You shall pour it out on the ground like water."

11. "You may convert them into money. Wrap up the money and take it with you to the place that the Lord your God has chosen."

12. "You shall not intermarry with them; do not give your daughters to their sons or take their daughters for your sons."

13. "In hot anger, may overtake him and kill him; yet he did not incur the death penalty, since he had never been the other's enemy."

# Fill In The Missing Words

1. "That …. doth not live by …. only."

2. "At the mouth of …. witnesses, or …. witnesses shall he that is to die be put to death."

3. "That which is gone out of thy …. thou shall observe and …."

4. "But …. waxed fat and …."

5. "But ye that …. unto the Lord your God are …. everyone of you this day."

6. "Ask thy father and he will …. unto thee, thine …. and they will tell thee."

7. "For a gift doth …. the eyes of …."

8. "How can I myself …. bear your cumbrance and your …. and your strife."

9. "Love you therefore the …., for you were strangers in the land of …."

10. One is not permitted to "muzzle an …. while it is …."

11. "The Lord thy God turned Balaam's …. into a …."

12. "You shall not take …., for they …. the eyes of the discerning and upset the plea of the just."

13. "You must …. what has crossed your lips and perform what you have voluntarily …."

14. "The …. acts belong unto the Lord our God, but the acts that are …. belong unto us and our children forever."

15. "Blessed shall you be in your …. and blessed shall you be in your …."

16. "Pay no heed unto the …. of this people, its …. and its sinfulness."

17. "This is the …. that …. set before the Israelites."

18. "They shall come out against thee …. way, and shall flee before thee …. ways."

19. "I call …. and …. to witness against you this day."

20. "And he forsook …. who made him, and spurned the …. of his salvation."

21. "A land whose stones are …. and out of whose hills thou mayest dig …."

22. "The …. shall not be put to death for the children, neither shall the …. be put to death for the fathers! Every man shall be put to death for his own sin."

# Identify The Following

1. "Behold his bedstead was a bedstead of iron."

2. "God hardened the heart of the king."

3. "He was buried in the valley in the land of Moab.

4. He got Gilead from Moses.

5. "Because he loved you and your house, because he fared well with you."

6. "He shall cause them to inherit the land."

7. One of the spies who "wholly followed the Lord."

8. "His first bullock, majesty is his."

9. He received the mountain of Seir as an inheritance."

10. "And he gave thee a sign or a wonder."

11. "Who regardeth not persons nor taketh reward."

12. They were swallowed by the earth.

13. A nation which attacked the Children of Israel while in the desert without any provocation.

14. Hired Balaam to curse the Children of Israel.

15. Did not eat or drink for forty days and forty nights.

16. A treasured people.

17. "The Lord is his inheritance. "

18. "Let him be the favored of his brethren."

19. "The beloved of the Lord shall dwell in safety by him."

20. "He dwelleth as a lioness, and teareth the arm, yea, the crown of the head."

21. "And upon the crown of the head of him that is prince among his brethren."

# Identify The Place

1. Mount Ebal

2. Edrei

3. Mount Grizim

4. Moserah

5. Valley of Eshcol

6. "Large cities with walls sky high."

7. "Took you and brought you out of .... that iron blast furnace..."

8. "The city of palm trees."

9. "For I will not give you any of their land as a possession; I have given .... as a possession to the descendants of Lot."

# Unique Questions

1. How do we recognize a kosher animal?

2. How do we recognize a kosher fish?

3. What are the seven kinds of choice products the Land of Israel was blessed with.

4. Name some of the laws concerning the Shmitah year.

5. "Remember the days of old, consider the years of ages past; Ask thy father, he will inform you, your elders, they will tell you" was said by whom and on what occasion?

6. We learn the concept of "ecology" from the Torah. Which trees in the Land are we forbidden to destroy, even in times of war and what is the reason given in the Torah?

7. For observing some commandments, the Torah promises long life as a reward. Name some of the commandments.

8. In the Torah we find laws that landowners are required to observe in order to provide for the poor, strangers, orphan, and widow. What are these provisions called?

9. Why were the Children of Israel told to blot out the memory of the Amalekites?

10. Give two examples of commandments in which the Torah commands us to have compassion for animals?

11. According to the Book of Deuteronomy, four types of men were exempt from going to war. Name three.

12. What did Moses make to protect the second set of the stone tablets?

13. Name the three "cities of refuge" east of the Jordan.

14. Name two of the "unclean" (non-kosher) birds listed in Deuteronomy.

15. Why does the Torah command us to build a parapet around the roof of a house?

16. What request did the Israelites make of Sihon, king of Bashan?

17. What attitude does the Torah take (in Deuteronomy) toward the practice of human sacrifice?

18. The Torah says that a person who "killeth his neighbor unawares" can flee to a city of refuge. What example of accidental manslaughter does the Torah give as an illustration?

19. What is the attitude of the Torah towards soothsayers, sorcerers, and those who consult ghosts and spirits?

20. What is to be done to the man who deliberately kills his neighbor and flees to a city of refuge?

21. Name the two mountains upon which the Children of Israel heard the blessings and curses?

22. In Deuteronomy, it is written: "And thou shalt bind them for a sign upon thy hand, and they shall be for frontlets between thine eyes." To what ritual object does this refer?

23. If your neighbor's donkey has fallen down, what does the Torah say you must do?

24. In the Book of Exodus, we find reasons for observing the Sabbath. What additional reasons are found in the Book of Deuteronomy?

25. What is a lender forbidden to do when he takes a pledge from the borrower?

26. Which nations did God advise the Children of Israel no to antagonize?

27. What are the two reasons given by the Torah not to admit "an Amonite or a Moabite, even to the tenth generation," into the congregation of Israel?

28. Why were the Children of Israel told not abhor an Edomite, or an Egyptian?

29. What passage from the Torah is written on the parchment inside the Mezuzah?

30. What is the Biblical quotation in regard to mixing meat and milk?

31. What passage in the Torah is the basis for Tzitzit?

32. Which event is always referred to as a reminder to the Israelites to be kind and just to the stranger?

33. The pursuit of justice is expressed tersely in Deuteronomy. (Three words in Hebrew, five words in English) What is the statement?

34. How is the fertility of the Land of Israel – as a land of milk and honey – described?

35. What statement in Deuteronomy teaches us that man needs more than normal sustenance?

36. What statement in Deuteronomy foretells that there will always be poor people?

37. What is our obligation to the body of a person who has been executed and why?

38. What does God promise to bring if the Israelites obey his commandments?

# Who Said What To Whom?

1. "Good is the land which the Lord our God gives to us"

2. "You shall pass over armed before your brethren."

3. "What man is there that is fearful and fainthearted?"

4. "The cause that is too hard for you ye shall bring unto me and I will hear it."

5. "I will make of thee a great nation mightier and greater than they."

6. "Cursed be he that taketh a bribe to slay an innocent person."

7. "He it is that doth go with thee; He will not fail thee, nor forsake thee."

8. "Also the Lord was angry with me for your sakes."

9. "I profess this day unto the Lord thy God, that I am come unto the Land."

10. "So shall it be done unto the man that doth not build up his brother's house."

11. "Get thee up into the top of Pisgah, and lift up thine eyes westward, and northward, and southward and eastward."

12. "Let me go over, I pray thee, and see the good land."

דברים

# Answers and Sources
# For The Questions
# From Genesis

# Multiple Choice

1. 400 shekels of silver; 23:15-17

2. Hagar from Sarah; 16:6

3. Jacob feared his brother Esau;     27:41-45

4. Jacob to the shepherds; 29:7

5. Enoch; 5:24

6. Noah; 6:9

7. Esau; 25:27

8. Ishmael; 16:12

9. Noah's Ark landed there; 8:4

10. The sixth day; 1:31

11. Reuben; 42:37

12. Dew of Heaven; 27:28-29

13. Abraham; 20:1-7

14. Enosh; 4:26

15. Reuben; 37:29-30

16. Shechem; 33:18-20

17. A marriage union; 24:49-51

18. The birthright; 25:34

19. A ladder reaching to the heavens; 28:12

20. He divided his family and flock into two camps; 32:8

21. Seven years of famine; 41:17-27

22. Seven days; 29:20-28

23. Was ten; 18:23-33

24. He will bury Jacob's body in Canaan; 47:29-31

25. Does my father yet live; 45:3

26. Judah; 43:8-9

27. Joseph; 42:9-14

28. Efrat; 35:19

29. Abraham; 20:4-5

30. Corn; 41:35

31. Good and Evil; 8:22

32. Grapes; 43:11

33. A dove; 8:2

34. Fish; 7:23

35. A silver bracelet; 41:42-43

36. To show that it would shortly be fulfilled; 41:32

37. Tamar; 38:24

38. Reuben; 37:29-30

39. Shimeon and Levi; 34: 25-26

40. Handmaidens, Leah, Rachel; 33:1-8

41. Twenty; 31:38

42. Joseph; 30:25-26

43. Aram Naharaim; 24:10

44. Bethuel; 24:15

45. Ishmael; 17:20

46. 400 years; 15:13

47. Isaac; 26:1-6

48. His grandfather; 11:26-27

49. Shinar; 11:2-9

50. Shepherd; 6:14, 9:20

בראשית

51. 150 days; 7:24

52. Nod; 4:16

53. Eve; 2:23

54. Alone; 2:18

55. Jacob's and Benjamin's; 43:27-30

56. Ten brothers; 42:13,42:32

57. Ten brothers; 42:24, 43:14, 23

58. Potiphar's; 39:11

59. Shela; 38:11

60. Dothan; 37:17

61. Bethel; 35:8

62. Erected an alter; 34:18-20

63. Esau; 32:12

64. Saddle; 31:34

65. Luz; 28:19

66. Abraham's servant to Bethuel; 24:33

67. Cave; 23:9-16

68. The wood; 22:6

69. Hagar; 16:7

70. Chedorlaomer; 14:13

71. Abraham and Isaac; 12:11-19, 26:6-9

72. To confound; 11:4-9

73. To 120; 6:3

74. Simeon; 42:24

75. Adam; 3:9

76. He informed him that his seed would be a stranger in a land that was not theirs, where they would be slaves for 400 years; 15:13

77. Because he was born in his old age; 37:3

78. That they should take his remains along with them when they left Egypt; 50:25

79. Israel; 48:10

80. Rachel; 48:7

81. The Euphrates River; 15:18

82. Laban and Jacob departed in a friendly manner; 31:23-35

83. The destruction of Sodom and Gomorrah; 18:25

84. Judah; 46:28

85. When Jacob left Laban going on the way to Canaan and prepared himself to meet Esau; 32:25

# About Whom Was This Said?

1. Esau; 25:27

2. Eliezer of Damascus; 15:2

3. Nimrod; 10:9

4. Tubal-Cain; 4:22

5. Joseph; 39:6

6. Shechem, son of Chamor; 34:7

7. Potiphar; 39:5

8. Joseph; 41:51

9. The brothers of Joseph; 42:28

10. Lot; 19:30

11. Jabal; 4:20

12. Ishmael; 16:12

13. Shem; 10:21

14. The butler and the baker; 40:7

15. Ephraim and Menashe; 48:16

16. Jubal; 4:21

17. Joseph; 42:7

# Who Did The Following?

1. Abraham; 14:21-23

2. Noah; 9:26

3. Abraham in Beer Sheba; 21:33

4. Jacob at Rachel's grave; 35:20

5. Malchizedek; 14:19

6. Abraham; 14:20

# Who Dreamed Of This?

1. The Chief Butler; 40:9-10

2. The Chief Baker; 40:16-17

3. Jacob; 28:12

4. Avimelech; 20:3-6

5. Joseph; 37:7

6. Pharaoh; 41:5

7. Laban; 31:24

# What Is The Correct Number?

1. Four; 19:16

2. 127; 23:1

3. 17 years; 37:2

4. 30 years; 41:46

5. 20 years; 31:34

6. 400 shekels; 23:16

7. Eight; 7:13

8. 60; 25:26

# Identify The Person With The Utensil

1. Joseph; 44:2

2. Chief Butler; 40:11

3. Rebecca; 24:17-37

4. Abraham; 22:10

5. Hagar; 21:16-19

6. Chief Baker; 40:17

# Who Said This To Whom?

1. God to Himself; 1:26

2. God to Himself; 2:18

3. God to Adam; 3:19

4. God to Adam; 3:19

5. Cain to God; 4:9

6. God to Cain; 4:12

7. Cain to God; 4:14

8. God to Noah; 9:13

9. God to Abraham; 12:2

10. God to Abraham; 12:3

11. Abraham to Lot; 13:8-9

12. Angel to Abraham; 22:12

13. Eliezer to Rebecca; 24:17

14. Laban and his mother to Eliezer; 24:57

15. Esau to Jacob; 25:30

16. Isaac to Esau; 27:28

17. Isaac to Esau; 27:40

18. Jacob to himself; 28:17

19. Jacob to God; 32:11

20. Joseph to a stranger; 37:16

21. Joseph's brothers to themselves; 37:19

22. Reuben to his brothers; 37:30

23. Chief Butler to Pharaoh; 41:9

24. Isaac to Jacob; 27:22

25. King of Sodom to Abraham; 14:21

26. Jacob to God; 32:12

27. Judah to his brothers; 37:26

28. Abraham to God; 18:26

29. Judah to Israel (Jacob); 43:9

30. Joseph to his brothers; 44:4

31. Abraham to Eliezer; 24:2

32. God to Abraham; 12:7

33. The Angel to Jacob; 32:25-29

34. The Angels to Lot; 19:1-15

35. Jacob to Rachel; 30:1-2

36. Butler to Pharaoh; 41:13

37. God to Laban 31:24

38. Rachel & Leah to Jacob; 31:15

39. Laban to Jacob; 29:15

40. Angel to Hagar; 16:12-13.

41. God to Noah and his sons; 9:6

42. Esau to Isaac; 27:38

43. Jacob to the Angel; 32:25-27

44. The Angel to Jacob; 32:27

45. Israel (Jacob) to Joseph; 48:11

46. Laban to Jacob; 31:48

47. Reuben to his brothers about Joseph; 37:21-22

48. Midwife to Rachel; 35:17

49. The butler to Pharaoh; 41:9

50. Rachel & Leah to Jacob; 31:14

51. Chamor & Shechem to their townsman; 34:21

52. Laban to Jacob; 29:14

# Who Does The Statement Refer To?

1. Noah; 7:1

2. Abraham; 12:1

3. Jacob; 25:27

4. Lot; 19:9

5. Malchizedek; 14:18

6. Ishmael; 21:20

7. Isaac; 26:14

8. Joseph; 42:7

9. Ephraim & Menashe; 48:13-16

10. Esau; 27:40

11. Isaac; 26:12

12. Noah to Japheth; 9:27

13. Isaac to Jacob; 27:29

14. Jacob to Ephraim & Menashe; 48:20

# Who Was The First...?

1. Cain; 4:2

2. Abel; 4:3

3. Jubal; 4:21

4. Tubal-Cain; 4:22

5. Eliezer; 24:4

6. Abraham; 12:1-5

7. Abraham; 12:19

8. Adam; 2:20

9. Noah; 6:9-20

10: Jacob; 32:29

11: Cain; 4:17

12. Tubal-Cain; 4:22

13. Laban; 29:21-25

14. Noah; 9:20

15. Noah; 9:21

16. Joseph; 37:28

17. Abraham; 12:10

# Match The Proverb With An Event

1. Abram dwelt in the land of Canaan and Lot dwelt in the cities of the Plain and his tent as far as Sodom.; 13:12

2. Let there be no strife, I pray thee, between me and thee, and between my herdsmen and thy herdsmen.; 13:8

3. And Joseph brought evil report of them unto their father.; 37:2

4. I will not take a thread, nor a shoe latchet, nor ought that is thine.; 14:22-23

5. With whomsoever thou findest thy gods, he shall not live.; 44:7-9

6. And when Abraham heard that his brother was taken captive, he led forth his trained men.; 14:14

7. I will fetch a morsel of bread and stay ye your hearts, after that ye shall stay on…and Abraham ran unto the herd and fetched a calf, tender and good.; 18:5-8

8. I am not worthy of all the mercies and of all the truth which Thou hast shown unto the servant.; 32:11

9. Deliver me, I pray Thee, O God, from the hand of my brother.; 32:12

10. Wilt Thou indeed sweep away and not forgive the place for the fifty righteous that are therein.; 18:24

# Unique Questions

1. Rachel, because she died on the road during the journey back to Canaan; 38:16-20

2. The Angel who struggled with him and named him Israel; 32;25-29

3. And there was evening and there was morning.; 1:5,8,13,19,23,31

4. Edom; 25:30

5. Rebecca; 24:65

6. His nephew, Lot; 14:14-16

7. Rebecca's nurse; 35:8

8. The animals entering Noah's Ark; 7:9

9. In Goshen; 47:27

10. Joseph & Benjamin; 30:24-35

11. Abraham & Sarah; 17:5-15

12. Bread & Pottage of lentils; 25:33-34

13. Jacob-Israel; 25:30, Esau-Edom; 32:29

14. Jacob; 37:34

15. a. Ishamael; 16:11, b. Isaac; 17:19

16. Rebecca; 24:58

17. Osnat; 41:45

18. His mother's brother and his father-in-law; 27:43

19. Metuselah, he lived 969 years; 5:29

20. On the way to Efrat, which is Bethlehem; 35:20

21. a. Rebecca; 24:15, b. Rachel; 29:9

22. a. Edom; 26:30, b. Israel; 32:28-29, c. Tzofnath-Paneach; 41:45

23. Malchizedek, king of Salem; 14:18

24. a. Abraham; 25:1, b. Nachor; 11:29, c. Esau; 26:35

25. On the third day of creation (Tuesday) the expression "and the Lord saw that it was good" is used twice, whereas on the other days of creation, the expression is used only once; 1:9-13

26. a. Seven days of the week; 2:1-2, b. Seven good and seven lean years in Egypt; 41:29-37, c. Seven days of mourning; 50:1-10

27. God promised to Abraham: "Unto thy seed will I give this land."; 12:7

28. With the sweat of your brow shall you eat bread.; 3:19

29. Be fruitful and multiply; 1:28

30. At the conclusion of the creation of the sixth day; 1:31

31. a. The donkey; 22:3, b. The camel; 24:11, c. The horse and wagon; 46:21

32. a. Forbidding idol worship; b. Adultery; c. Bloodshed; d. Cutting the limb of a live animal; e. Profaning God; f. Stealing; g. Laws between man and man; 9:1-7

33. Jacob's family. The daughter's name was Dinah; 30:1-21

34. Reuben – cast him into the pit; 37:22, Judah – come and let us sell him to the Ishmaelites; 37:27

35. a. Abraham-Sarah; 12:11-13, b. Isaac-Rebecca; 26:7

36. a. Noah's Ark rested there; 8:4, b. The binding of Isaac; 22:2

37. a. Nimrod; 10:9, b. Esau; 25:27, c. Ishmael; 16:12

38. The daughters are my daughters, and the children are my children, and the flocks are my flocks, and all that you see is mine.; 31:43

39. Jacob to Joseph; 48:19

40. a. Wolf; 49:27, b. Lion; 49:9, c. Hind; 49:21, d. Snake; 49:17

41. a. Abraham-Hebron, Cave of Machpelah; 23:17, b. Jacob, near Shechem; 33:19

42. God be gracious unto thee, my son.; 43;29

43. a. Luz; 28:19, b. Efrat; 35:19, c. Kiryat Arba; 23:2

44. Abraham put up a tent between Bethel and Ai; 12:8

45. Dan; 49:18

46. I will go down with thee into Egypt and also surely bring thee up again.; 46:4

47. a. Abraham; 20:7, b. Joseph; 41:38, c. Abraham; 23:6

48. a. Reuben; 49:3, b. Simeon; 49:5, c. Levi; 49:5

49. a. Foreign gods; 35:4, b. Earrings; 35:4

50. a. 300 shekels of silver; 45:22, b. 5 changes of raiment; 45:22

51. a. Asenath; 41:50-51, b. Tamar; 38:29-30, c. Leah; 30:21

52. a. Abraham-99 years old; 17:24, b. Isaac-8 days old; 21:4, c. Ishmael-13 years; 17:25

53. a. The baker; 40:16, b. Jacob; 31:12, c. Joseph; 37:7, d. Pharaoh; 41:5, e) The butler; 40:10

54. a. God made a covenant with Abraham; b. "And in the fourth generation, they shall come back hither." 15:16

55. He overheard their conversation in Hebrew: "We are verily guilty concerning our brother in that we saw the distress of his soul."; 42:21

56. a. During the flood, it rained for 40 days; 7:4, b. Jacob's embalmment; 50:2-3

57. The land of the Hebrews; 40:15

58. a. Malchizedek offered to give Abraham a tenth of all spoils; 14:20, b. Jacob said to God on the way to Charan: "I will surely give the tenth unto thee."; 28:22

59. Jacob divided his family and flock into two camps; 32:8

60. Abraham; 16:13, Joseph; 41:50

# Give The Blessing Jacob Gave To These Sons

1. A fruitful vine by a fountain, its branches run over the wall; 49:22

2. A wolf that raveneth, in the morning he devoureth the prey; 49:27

3. He shall be a serpent on the way, a horned snake in the path; 49:17

4. He shall dwell at the shore of the sea and he shall be a shore for ships; 49:13

5. He crouched as a lion, and as a lioness who shall rouse him up; 49:9

6. Unstable as water, have not thou the excellency; 49:4

7. A hind let loose, he giveth goodly words; 49:21

8. His bread shall be fat, and he shall yield royal dainties; 49:20

בראשית

# Who Were These People?

1. Friend of Abraham; 14:13

2. King of Salem; 14:18

3. Avimelech's captain; 26:26

4. Rebecca's nurse; 35:8

# Identify These Places

1. Avram's birthplace; 11:31

2. Where Laban dwelt; 29:4

3. Where Jacob bought a field; 33:19

4. Where Sarah died; 23:2

# What Story Is Connected With The Following:

1. Jacob gave Joseph a coat of many colors, which aroused the anger and hatred of his brothers. 37:3

2. Benjamin, Jacob's youngest son, was accused by his brother Joseph in Egypt of stealing his goblet. 44:1-12

3. Mount Moriah is connected with Abraham and Isaac, and later the site of the Holy Temple in Jerusalem. 22:1-3

4. Jacob, in his dream, saw a ladder reaching to heaven, and angels ascending and descending on it. 28:10-12

5. Pharaoh's Chief Baker saw in his dreams three baskets with baked goods. 40:16-17

בראשית

# In What Events Were These Expressions Used?

1. Mourning for Jacob; 50:10

2. Joseph's brothers; 37:18

3. Prepared for Isaac; 27:7

4. Reuben; 49:4

5. Blessing of Asher; 49:20

6. Shepherds; 46:34

7. Pharaoh's Question; 46:33

8. Purchase of Machpelah; 23:6

9. Cherubim; 3:24

10. Jacob wrestled with the angel; 32:33

# Answers and Sources
# For The Questions
# From Exodus

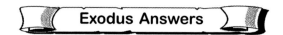

# Multiple Choice

1. Because she took pity on him; 2:6

2. This month shall be unto you the beginning of months; 12:2

3. When they lacked water; 17:4

4. Men of kindness; 18:21

5. Honor thy father and mother; 20:12

6. He pays double; 22:8

7. From twenty years and up; 30:14

8. Fleeing to a city of refuge; 21:13

9. Because God rested on the seventh day; 20:11

10. Rosh Hashanah; 23:15-16

11. The same day when the sun goes down; 22:25

12. Joseph; 1:1-5

13. He who made his servants and his cattle flee into the house; 9:20

14. The show bread; 25:30

15. Hail; 9:22-24

16. Soot of the furnace; 9:8-10

17. Locust; 10:12-15

18. The Egyptians; 10:21-23

19. The sons of Levi; 32:26-28

20. Son of Moses; 3:21,22

21. A dog; 11:4-7

22. When a Hebrew slave does not want to go free; 21:2-6

23. Fourth; 20:5

24. You shall restore it to him by the time the sun goes down; 22:24-26

שמות

25. Of Acacia wood; 25:10

26. Donkey; 24:20

27. Aviv; 13:4

28. You shall surely bring it back to him again; 23:4

29. The daughter of Levi; 2:1

30. His sister; 2:4

31. Who am I that I should go unto Pharaoh? ; 3:11

32. Of Joseph; 13:19

33. The feast of the harvest; 23:16

34. The table in the Tabernacle; 25:23

35. The ephod; 28:40

36. Holy to the Lord; 28:36

37. The tribe of Levi; 32-36

38. They spun the goat's hair ; 35:36

39. Amalek; 17:8

40. To appoint judges; 18:21

41. Girgashite; 3:8

42. Frogs; 8:5

43. At the red sea, 14:11

44. Men of charitable deed; 18:21

45. Thou shalt not covet; 20:14

46. When his master smites out his eye or tooth; 21:26-27

47. The Golden Calf; 32:20

48. Because this would cause the Children of Israel to sin; 23:23

49. I will bring you, I will deliver, I will redeem, I will take; 6:6-8

50. An omerful of manna; 16:32

ש

מ

ו

ת

51. Named his son Eliezer; 18:4

52. Five times its value; 21:37

53. They suffered from impatience of spirit and cruel bondage; 6:9

54. The half shekel; 30:15

55. They feared God; 1:17

56. Long life; 20:12

57. After seven years; 21:2

# Who Did The Following?

1. Pharaoh; 8:11

2. Pharaoh's daughter; 2:5

3. Aaron; 32:4

4. Joshua; 33:11

5. Bezalel; 37:12

6. Jethro; 18:9

7. Miriam; 15:20

8. Young men of Israel; 24:5

9. Amalek; 17:8

10. Moses; 17:12

11. Moses; 34:34

12. Zipporah; 4:25

13. Pharaoh; 9:34

14. Joseph; 13:19

15. Pharaoh; 14:6

ש

מ

ו

ת

# Fill In The Missing Words

1. Multitude...evil; 23:2

2. Widow...fatherless; 22:21

3. Wicked...witness; 23:1

4. Do...obey; 24:7

5. Light...dwelling; 12:23

6. Hand...prevailed; 17:11

7. Strength...salvation; 15:2

8. Thee...mighty; 15:11

9. Kingdom...nation; 19:6

10. Oppress... strangers; 22:20

11. Blessed...hallowed; 20:11

12. Seethe... milk; 23:19

13. Burned...consumed; 3:2

14. Shoes...holy; 3:5

15. People...wilderness; 5:1

16. You...strangers; 12:49

17. Raised...Israel; 17:11

18. Willing...offering; 25:2

19. Mastery... overcome; 32:18

20. Tree...waters; 15:25

21. Tables...law; 24:12

22. Sight...righteous; 23:8

23. Far...slay; 23:7

שמרה

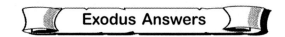

## Match The Following Names

1. Eliezer; 18:4

2. Kohath; 6:18

3. Pinchas; 6:25

4. Aminadab; 6:23

5. Oholiab; 31:6

6. Nachshon; 6:23

7. Ithamar; 6:23

8. Shifra; 1:15-17

9. Joshua; 33:11

# What Stories Or Events
# Are Connected With The Following?

1. The basket in which Moses was placed on the Nile; 2:24

2. The rod of Moses with which he performed signs and wonders before Pharaoh; 4:1-5, 7:9-18

3. Miriam the prophetess, the sister of Aaron, took a timbrel in her hand, and all the women went out after her with timbrels and with dances; 15:20

4. God told Moses to tell the Israelites as they stood at Mount Sinai "I bore you on eagles"; 19:3-6

5. The Children of Israel were instructed to take a jar and put an omer full of manna therein and lay it up before the Lord, to be kept throughout the generations; 16:33

6. A pillar of cloud guided the Israelites by day and a pillar of fire by night; 13:21

7. Thou shall not cook a kid in its mother's milk; 23:19

שׁ

מ

ו

ת

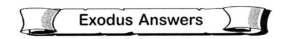

# What Happened At These Places?

1. God appeared there in the midst of a bush; 3:1

2. On the shore of the Red Sea; 14:2

3. Moses threw a tree into the water; 15:23-25

4. The first stop for the Children of Israel in the desert; 12:37

5. The Children of Israel lived there in Egypt; 9:26

# What Is The Law?

1. Redeem him; 13:13

2. Redeem him with a lamb; 13:13

3. You shall surely release it with him; 23:5

4. The ox shall surely be stoned; 21:28

5. Pay thirty shekels to the master; 21:32

# Match The Places

1. Rephidim; 17:8

2. Midian; 2:15

3. Sukkot; 12:37]

4. Mount Horeb; 3:1

5. Elim; 15:27

6. Marah; 15:25

7. Wilderness of Sin; 16:1

8. Red Sea; 23:31

9. Sea of Philistines; 23:31

שׁ

מ

ו

ת

# About Whom Or What Was It Said?

1. Widow or orphan; 22:22

2. God's Angel; 23:21

3. Aaron; 4:14

4. Garment as pledge; 22:25

5. A Hebrew slave; 21:3

6. Locust; 10:19

7. Half-shekel; 30:15

8. Tefillin; 13:16

9. Locust; 10:15

10. Pascal Lamb; 12:10

11. Flesh torn by a beast; 22:30

12. Cherubim; 25:20

13. Bezalel; 35:31

14. The Red Sea; 14:27

15. Willful murderer; 21:14

16. Aaron; 4:16

17. By the officers of the Children of Israel; 5:16

18. Moses' hand; 4:7

19. Anointing oil; 30:32

20. Soot of the furnace; 9:8

21. Quail; 16:13

22. Locust; 10:15

23. Manna; 16:31

24. First night of Passover; 12:42

שמות

# Who Said To Whom?

1. God to Moses; 4:14

2. Jethro to his daughters; 2:20

3. Magicians of Pharaoh when they could not duplicate one of the ten plagues. (Gnats) 8:15

4. Moses to a Hebrew slave; 2:11-15

5. A Hebrew slave to Moses because he did not like Moses interfering in his quarrel with another Hebrew slave; 2:11-15

6. Aaron said this to the Israelites after he made the Golden Calf from the gold the people gave him for this purpose; 32:1-6

7. Moses to Jethro; 4:18

8. Jethro to Moses; 18:21

9. Jethro's daughters to Jethro; 2:19

10. Pharaoh to Moses and Aaron; 5:2

11. Moses to God; 32:32

12. Pharaoh to his People; 1:10

13. Moses to the people of Israel; 32:26

14. Pharaoh to Moses and Aaron; 5:4

15. Moses to the people; 16:25

16. Moses to the people; 16:19

17. Joseph to the Children of Israel; 13:19

18. The Children of Israel to Moses; 14:11

19. Pharaoh's servants to the king; 10:7

20. God to Moses; 17:14

21. Joshua to Moses; 32:17

22. Pharaoh to his people; 14:13

ש

מ

ו

ת

23. Pharaoh to the taskmasters; 5:9

24. Jethro to Moses; 18:18

25. Pharaoh to Moses; 10:8

26. Moses to God; 4:13

27. Pharaoh to officers of the Children of Israel; 5:17

# Unique Questions

1. a. Passover- Exodus from Egypt; 12:21-42  b. Shavuot- The giving of the Torah at Mount Sinai; 19:1 c. Sukkot- The journey in the desert enroute to the Promised Land; 23:42-44

2. In the burning bush; 3:1-7

3. The Manna; 16:14-19

4. As a land flowing with mild and honey; 13:5

5. It is the Sabbath when the crossing of the red sea is read in the synagogue and the passage beginning "Then Moses sang unto the Lord"; 15:1-19

6. He was concerned of the battle with the Philistines who live along the coast of Canaan; 13:17

7. a. The Ten Commandments; 20:1-14  b. The ten plagues; 7:8:9:10:11  c. Joseph's ten brothers who came down to Egypt the first time; 42:3

8. Pharaoh's daughter when she found him in the river.  Because the word Moses means to draw from or fetch; 2:10

9. The story of the burning bush; 3:1-5

10. The enslavement and harsh treatment of the Israelites in Egypt; 5:16

11. Aaron his brother; 4:10-16, 6:29-30, 7:1-2

12. The Israelites should always remember that they were strangers in Egypt; 23:9

13. Aaron; 32:1-4

14. Moses did not drink or eat for 40 days while on Mount Sinai; 34:28

15. The Sabbath is an eternal covenant between the Jewish People and God; 31:13

16. Egypt is characterized as the "House of Bondage"; 20:1

17. By day, a pillar of cloud and by night a pillar of fire; 13:21-22

18. A slave who did not wish to be freed from slavery was brought by his master before a judge and has his ear pierced as a sign that he would serve forever (until the Jubilee year); 21:1-6

19. "Honor thy father and thy mother" is the fifth commandment; 20:12

20. The source for the eternal light is in a statement: "And thou shalt command the Children of Israel that they bring unto thee pure olive oil beaten for the light, to cause a lamp to burn continually"; 27:20-21

21. The Israelites are described as "A stiff necked people"; 34:9

22. The Israelites built Pithom and Raamses for the Egyptians during their enslavement; 1:11-14

23. The Israelites when Moses presented to them the commandments, laws and statutes; 24:7

24. It refers to Passover; 12:11

25. On Friday (the sixth day of the week) the Israelites gathered twice as much manna for each person; 16:22

26. To Midian; 2:15

27. Moses; 2:6

28. Shifrah and Puah; 1:15

29. The tefillin; 13:9

30. Wafers made with honey; 16:31

31. a. Pesach- feast of the unleavened bread. b. Shavuot- feast of the harvest. c. Sukkot – Feast of the Ingathering; 23:14-17

32. Mount Horeb; 3:1-2

33. And the Egyptians dug around about the river (Nile) for water to drink; 7:24

34. Zipporah; 2:21

שׁ

מ

ו

ת

35. The Philistines; 13:17

36. The first night of Passover; 12:42

37. To the Jewish people; 19:6

38. Six Hundred Thousand; 12:37

39. Payment of double, fourfold, or fivefold; 21:37, 22:3

40. Deliberate murder; 21:14

41. The first two – blood and frogs; 7:22, 8:3

42. Nadav, Avihu, Elazar, Ithamar; 28:1

43. (Ohel Moed) The tent of meeting; 33:7

44. Jethro; 18:9

45. Four hundred and thirty years; 12:40

46. Seventy, six hundred thousand; 1:5, 12:37

47. A three day rest in the desert to worship God; 5:3

48. "I am that I am"; 3:14

49. Because his face sent forth beams of light; 34:29

50. The owner of the pit shall make it good, he shall give money to the owner of the animal, and the dead animal shall be his; 21:33-34

51. Long life; 20:21

52. A half a shekel was given by every male person over age 20; 30:11-15

53. The names of the tribes of Israel; 28:29

54. a. The flax and barley were smitten because they were ripe (for the barley was in the bar and the flax was in the bloom). b. The wheat and spelt were not smitten because they were not ripe (for they ripen late); 9:31,32

55. a. Chag HaMatzot – feast of unleavened bread. b. Chag HaBikurim – feast of harvest. c. Chag HaAsif – Feast of the ingathering; 23:15-16

56. a. Philistia b. Moab c. Edom d. Canaan; 15:14-15

57. a. Burnt it. b. Ground it into powder. c. Strewed it upon the water. d. Made the Israelites drink it; 32:20

58. a. The east wind brought the locust. b. The east wind blew all night and made the Red Sea dry land; 10:13, 14:21

59. a. Ark. b. Table. c. Menorah; 25:10, 23:31

60. a. At the plague of the first-born. There it says: "but against any of the Children of Israel shall not a dog whet its tongue. b. "Meat torn of beasts, ye shall cast it to the dogs"; 11:7, 22:30

61. Through Aaron; 7:19, 8:1

62. Midian; 2:22

63. a. Elazar – son of Aaron; 6:23. b. Eliezer – son of Moses; 18:4

64. a. Moses judged the people; 18:14. b. The Israelites ate the pascal lamb; 12:8-10

65. a. The pascal lamb- they were told to keep it for four days; 12:3-6. b. The Manna-only until morning; 16:16-19. c. A jar filled with manna as a memorial for all generations; 16:33

66. a. Swarms; 8:27 b. Locust; 10:19 c. The Egyptians who pursued the Israelites; 14:28

67. a. Aaron. b. Hur (the son of Miriam); 17:2

68. a. Unleavened Bread. b. Bitter Herbs; 12:8

69. a. Breastplate. b. Ephod. c. Robe. d. Tunic, Nitre, Girdle, Plate of Gold, Breeches; 28.

70. a. Gershom: "I have been a stranger in a strange land" b. Eliezer: "For the God of my father was my help and delivered me from the sword of Pharoah";18:3-4

71. "Seven days shall there be no leaven found in your houses" and "There shall no leavened bread be seen with you, neither shall there be leaven seen in all your borders";12:19

72. a. Jewels of silver. b. Jewels of Gold. c. Raiment; 12:35

73. a. Your loin girded. b. Your shoes on your feet. c. Your staff in your hand. d. You shall eat in haste; 12:11

74. That which pertains to the eating of food. "Save that which every man must eat, that only may be done by you."; 12:16

ש

מ

ו

ת

75. a. Like a stone. b. As stubble. c. As lead; 15:5,7,10

76. The sound of the golden bells; 28:34-35

77. The convocation at Sinai; 19:11

שׁ

מ

ו

ת

# Answers and Sources
# For The Questions
# From Leviticus

# Multiple Choice

1. a. As a remembrance that the Children of Israel dwelled in Sukkot in the wilderness; 23:42

2. d. In the first month (Nissan) on the 15th day; 23:6

3. a. The poor and stranger; 19:9-10

4. b. The seventh year; 25:2-7

5. c. Because the Children of Israel are the Servants of God; 25:42

6. b. Fellow citizens; 19:33-34

7. d. Holding back wages of a hired servant; 19:13

8. c. One who blasphemed God, because it was unclear how to punish him; 24:12

9. b. Earthen vessels; 11:33

10. d. On the fifth; 19:23-25

11. b. Yom Kippur; 23:27

12. d. All citizens or residents of Israel; 23:42

13. b. Yom Kippur; 25:9

14. d. Sukkot; 23:40

15. b. Pure olive oil; 24:2

16. c. Land; 25:23

17. b. Your neighbor; 19:13

18. d. On Yom Kippur that falls in the Jubilee year; 25:9

19. b. To Keep the Sabbath; 19:3

20. c. Tattooing; 19:28

21. b. It parts its hoof, is cloven footed, and chews the cud; 11:2-9

22. c. An abundant crop in the sixth year; 25:20-23

23. a. The camel; 11:2-9

24. d. Levites; 25:23-34

25. b. All winged things that go upon all fours, which have jointed legs for leaping upon the ground; 11:13-23

26. d. He kept quiet; 10:3

27. a. A new meal offering; 23:16

28. b. As a home-born of the land; 19:33-34

29. a. He shall be cut off from his people; 23:16

30. b. Rosh Hashanah; 23:24-25

31. c. The stranger; 19:33

32. a. Yom Kippur; 23:32

33. c. Fins and scales; 11:9

# Fill In The Missing Words

1. vintage...sowing; 26:5

2. hate...rebuke; 19:17

3. aged...old; 19:32

4. deaf...blind; 19:14

5. liberty...inhabitants; 25:10

6. unrighteousness...weight; 19:35

7. jubilee...man; 25:13

8. law...home-born; 24:22

9. hundred...ten thousand; 26:8

10. peace...afraid; 26:6

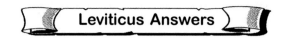

## About What Or Whom Was It Said?

1. The High Priest; 21:10-13

2. The son of the Israelitish women; 24:10-12

3. Jubilee year; 25:10-11

4. Your brother; 19:18

5. The stranger; 19:34

6. The grain; 26:10

## To What Or To Whom Is Referred?

1. The length of the Yom Kippur fast; 23:23

2. To set the permanent lamp; 24:3

3. The Jubilee year; 25:8

4. The holiday of the first fruits; 23:15-21

5. The Etrog; 23:40

6. The Myrtle; 23:40

7. A blessing for the fruits; 26:4

8. The blasphemer; 24:13-14

9. The slave; 25:53

10. A Hebrew slave; 25:47-53

## Who Said To Whom?

1. Moses to Mishael and Elzaphan; 10:4

2. God to Aaron; 10: 8-9

## Identify The Person

1. Nadav and Avihu; 10:1

2. Elazar and Itamar; 10:16

3. Aaron; 10:3

## Unique Questions

1. "Proclaim Liberty throughout the land unto all the inhabitants thereof"; 25:10

2. "Love your neighbor as yourself"; 19:18

3. The seventh year was known as the *Shmitah* (Sabbatical) year during which there was no planting. The fiftieth year was known as the *Yovel* (Jubilee) year, at which time land was released to the original owners and slaves were freed; 25:2-24

4. In order to help the poor, the Torah tells us: "And when you reap the harvest of your land, you shall not wholly reap the corner of your field, neither shall you gather the gleaning of the harvest. And you shall not glean your vineyard, neither shall you gather the fallen fruit of your vineyard. You shall leave them for the poor and for the stranger."; 19:9-10

5. The Torah tells us: "And you shall take for you on the first day the fruit of goodly trees, branches of palm trees, and boughs of thick trees, and willows of the brook, and you shall rejoice before the Lord your God seven days."; 23:40

6. The Shofar (the horn): "Then shall you make a proclamation with the horn."; 25:9

7. a. The fruit of the trees that grows during the fourth year is holy to the Lord;

b. Fruit of the tree that is permitted to eat during the fifth year;

c. In the sixth year there will be a blessing for an extra harvest to make up for the fallow seventh year; 25:21

8. a. House in walled city-i.e. urban dwelling; 25:30:  b. Levite property; 25:33:
   c. Fields-open land belonging to the Levites; 25:34

ו

ד

ק

ד

א

9. Because the land belongs to God; 25:23

10. a. The fourteenth day of the first month;  b. The first day of the seventh month;  c. The tenth day of the seventh month; The fifteenth day of the seventh month; 23:4-44

11. "Just balances, just weights, a just *epha*, and a just *hin* shall you have"; 19:36

12. "If your brother be waxen poor with you and sells himself to you"; 25:39

13. In the Book of Leviticus in the *"Tochacha"* the Israelites are warned that if they do not follow the commandments they will be punished: "I will make your heaven as iron and your earth as brass"; 26:19

14. a. You shall do no unrighteousness in judgment, you shall not respect the person of the poor nor favor the person of the mighty, but in righteousness shall you judge your neighbor; 19:15:

b. You shall have one manner of law, as well for the stranger as for the home-born; 24:22

15. The stranger; 19:34

16. a. Lulav-Etrog-Hadassim-Aravah; 23:39-40:

b. "The fruit of goodly trees, branches of palm trees, and boughs of thick trees, and willows of the brook; 23:39-40

17. It should be paid at once, not kept overnight; 19:40

18. The High Priest; 8:6-8

19. Nadav and Avihu, the sons of Aaron, were devoured by fire; 10:1-2

20. On the eighth day after birth; 12:3

21. The Kohanim – the Priests; 13:1

22. The blood: "For the life of the flesh is in the blood"; 17:10-11

23. The Torah tells us: "You shall fear every man, his mother and his father"; 19:3

24. "You shall rise up before the aged and show deference to the old"; 19:32

25. "Do not deal basely with your fellows. Do not profit by the blood of your neighbor" 19:16

ו

ד

ק

ר

א

26. "None shall defile himself for any (dead person among his people, except for the relatives that are closest to him: His mother, his father, his son, his daughter, and brother, and for a virgin sister"; 21:1-3

27. "He shall not go in where there is any dead body; he shall not defile himself even to his father or mother"; 21:11

28. The blasphemer was put to death by stoning; 24:10-16

29. It is a reward: "If you follow my laws and faithfully observe my commandments...you shall give chase to your enemies...five of you shall give chase to a hundred and a hundred of you shall give chase to ten thousand"; 26:3-8

30. a. "Any Israelite or a stranger residing in Israel who gives any of his offsprings to Molech, shall be put to death"; 20:1-2:

b. The goat over which the High Priest confessed on Yom Kippur all the iniquities and transgressions of the Israelites – and was sent off to the wilderness; 16:21-26

31. a. The counting of the Omer: "And from the day on which you bring the sheaf of wave offering-the day after the Sabbath-you shall count seven weeks"; 23:15:

b. The Sabbatical year: "In the seventh year the land shall have a Sabbath of complete rest, a Sabbath of the Lord" 25:4:

c. Jubilee: "You shall count of seven weeks of years, seven times seven years...A total of forty-nine years...and you shall hallow the fiftieth year...It shall be a Jubilee"; 25:8-10

32. "You shall not curse the deaf, and place a stumbling block before the blind"; 19:14

33. One should rebuke his neighbor with delicacy and tact; 19:17

34. "Shabbat Shabbaton" – It is a Sabbath of solemn rest to you and you shall afflict your souls"; 16:31

35. The Kohanim; 10:8-9

36. "If any man insults his father or his mother, he shall be put to death"; 20:9

37. "You shall not follow the practices of the nations that I am driving out before

you. For it is because they did all these things that I abhorred them"; 20:23

38. "The Priest who is exalted above his fellows, on whose head the anointing oil has been poured on his head"; 8:12

39. "No man among the offsprings of Aaron the Priest who has a defect shall be qualified to offer offerings to God"; 21:21

40. Lighting the menorah daily was the responsibility of Aaron; 24:1-3

# Answers and Sources
# For The Questions
# From Numbers

# Multiple Choice

1. Inheritance; 27:9

2. On the day of the first fruits (Shavuot); 28:26

3. The division of the Land of Israel; 33:54

4. The cities of refuge; 35:8

5. Inheritance of the Israelites shall not be removed from tribe to tribe; 36:7

6. The laws of manslaughter; 35:28

7. It was God who appointed Aaron to the High Priesthood; 17:20

8. The blessings of Balaam; 24:5

9. The Priestly Benediction; 6:26

10. The craving for eating meat; 11:32-34

11. The Israelites went to war without Moses' permission; 14:45

12. The war of Midian; 31:23

13. Passover; 9:1-14

14. The land of Egypt; 16:12-13

15. The first-born among the Children of Israel; 3:12

16. A cluster of grapes, pomegranates, and figs; 13:23

17. To Kiriath-Chutzoth; 22:39

18. In the war with Midian; 31:6

19. By passing them into fire; 31:21-23

20. Sheepfolds for their cattle and cities for their families; 32: 16:24

21. He was very humble above all the men that were of the face of the earth; 12:3

22. "Heal her now, O God, I beseech Thee"; 12:13

23. Because they rebelled against God at the waters of Meribah; 20:23-24

24. To appoint a leader over the people to replace him.; 27:15-18

25. That they will be the vanguard of the army until they subdue the enemy; 32: 20-23

26. Because she spoke against Moses; 12:1-3

27. To carry the Tabernacle and its vessels and to guard them; 3:5-10

28. 48 cities; 35:7

29. Part of the instructions given to the spies; 13:17-18

30. God; 9:15-21

31. Every sacred object is to be carried on the shoulders; 7:9

32. The people took to complaining bitterly before God; 11:1

33. A man's wife who goes astray; 5:18

34. In Balaam's blessing; 24:7

35. The redemption of the first-born; 18:16

36. The man gathering sticks; 15:34

37. Daily offerings; 28:2

38. Nose rings; 31:50

39. Reuben; 2:3-10

40. Inheritance of the Israelites shall not be removed from tribe to tribe; 36:7

41. From age 30 and up; 4:23

42. Tithes; 18:21

43. One tenth of the tithe is given by the Levites to the Kohen; 18:26-28

44. A man's wife who goes astray; 5:2

45. The red heifer; 19:6

46. No stranger may offer incense before God; 17:5

47. Elazar; 20:28

48. The king of Edom; 20:14

במדבר

49. The camp of Dan; 10:25

50. No one – it is binding; 30:10

51. Upon the death of the High Priest; 35:28

52. The waters at Meribah; 20:10

53. He was granted a covenant for an everlasting priesthood; 25:13

54. The camp of Judah; 10:14

55. From age 20; 1:3

56. The fiery serpents; 21:7

57. He rebelled against God's word at the waters of Meribah; 20:24

58. His brothers; 27:9

59. The 70 Elders; 11:16

60. Rebellion of Korach; 16:22

61. Fleeing to the city of refuge; 35:11

62. To the tribes of Gad and Reuben; 32:14

63. His sin is not stated in the Torah; 27:3

64. The rod of Aaron; 17:25

65. Because the land there was fertile and good for grazing, and they had lots of cattle; 32:1

66. Because they complained about the manna and lack of bread and water; 21:5

67. The reports of the spies; 14:22

68. So that no inheritance shall be moved from tribe to tribe; 36:6-7

69. The eating of the meat; 11:4

70. The quail; 11:33-34

71. On the day of the first fruits (Shavuot); 28:26

72. Ages 25-50; 8:24

73. Fasting; 6:2-21

במדבר

74. He was unclean by reason of a dead body; 9:10-11

75. By blowing two silver trumpets; 10:2

76. To choose a captain and return to Egypt; 14:4

77. The little ones; 14:31

# About Whom Or What Is It Said

1. Moses; 11:29

2. Pinchas; 25:11

3. Manna; 11:7

4. Og; 21:34

5. Zelophechad; 27:3

6. Joshua; 27:18

7. God to Moses; 11:23

8. About Moses; 12:7

9. The Angel of God; 22:32

10. The Manna; 11:7-8

11. The Elders of Midian and Moab; 22:7

12. The Spies; 13:23

13. The Rod of Aaron; 17:23

14. The Manslayer; 35:25

15. The two and half tribes of Reuben, Gad, and Menashe; 34:15

16. Balaam; 24:1

17. The spies; 13:25

18. Tzitzit-the fringes on corners of the garment; 15:39

19. Husband of straying wife; 5:14

במדבר

20. The first yield of your baking; 15:20

21. A red heifer; 19:2

22. An angel; 22:23

23. Elazar; 27:21

24. Balak; 24:10

25. The Pascal lamb; 9:12

26. Caleb; 14:24

27. Joshua; 27:18

28. The Nazarite; 6:5

29. The serpent; 21:8

30. Aaron's rod; 17:23

31. The Levites; 8:16

32. The spies; 13:33

33. Dathan and Aviram; 16:27-30

# Who Are They?

1. Miriam; 12:1

2. Joshua; 13:16

3. Zimri; 25:14

4. Zelophechad; 27:1

5. Elazar; 20:26

6. A Nazarite; 6:7

7. The tribe of Levi; 1:49

8. King of Arad; 21:1

9. Pinchas; 25:7

10. Balaam; 24:1

11. The spies; 13:26

12. Edom; 20:21

13. Nadav and Avihu; 3:4

# Who Said To Whom?

1. Aaron to Moses; 12:11

2. Moses to his father-in-law; 10:29

3. God to Aaron and Miriam; 12:8

4. The spies to the Children of Israel; 13:32

5. Edom to the Children of Israel; 20:18

6. Joshua and Caleb to the Children of Israel; 20:18

7. Balak to Balaam; 22:37

8. Moses to God; 16:15

9. Korach and his company to Moses; 16:3

10. The tribes of Gad and Reuben; 32:25

11. Moses to God; 11:23

12. The donkey to Balaam; 22:30

13. The High Priest (Kohen) to the straying wife; 5:21

14. God to Moses; 31:2

15. Balak to Balaam; 22:37

16. The donkey to Balaam; 22:30

17. Moses to the tribes of Gad and Reuben; 32:22

18. Hobab (Jethro) to Moses; 10: 30

19. Moses to Hobab; 10:31

במדבר

20. Balaam to the donkey; 22:29

21. God to Balaam; 22:9

22. God to Moses; 25:12

23. Balak to Balaam; 22:37

24. Moses to the tribes of Gad and Reuben; 32:6

25. Moses to Joshua; 11:29

26. Moses to the king of Edom; 20:14

27. One Israelite to another; 14:14

28. The mixed multitude to Moses; 11:4-5

29. Moses to God; 11:12

30. Caleb to the Israelites; 13:30

# Unique Questions

1. a. Midianite; 10:29     b. Canaanite; 21:1    c. Amorite; 21:21

2. a. Moses; 12:7     b. Caleb; 14:24

3. a. Aaron, with a fire pan with incense; 17:12-13    b. Pinchas, by killing Zimri and Cozbi; 25: 7-9

4. a. The spies sent by Moses; 13:33    b. Miriam's leprosy; 12:10   c. The manna; 11:7    d. The people of Israel; 23:24

5. a. The shutting away of Miriam; 12:15     b. The spying of the Land; 13:25 c. The eating of meat; 11:20

6. a. "How be it the people that dwell in the land are fierce and the cities are fortified and very great; and moreover we saw the Children of Anak there." b. "A land that eateth up its inhabitants." c. "All the people that we saw in it are men of great stature."; 13:22-32

במדבר

7. a. Sichon, "And came Jahaz and fought against Israel"; 21:23    b. Og, "And Og the King of Bashan...to battle at Edrei."; 21:33    c. Balak, "And he sent messengers...curse Me this people"; 25:5-6

8. a. "We should go up and possess it"; 13:30    b. "It is an exceedingly good land, a land which flowed with milk and honey"; 14:7

9. a. The mountain of Avarim – Moses; 27:12    b. Kiriath-Chutzoth-Balaam; 22:39

10. a. "Lo it is a people that shall dwell alone, and shall not be reckoned among the nations"; 23:9 b. "Behold a people that rises up like a lioness, and as a lion does he lift himself up"; 23:24    c. "How goodly are thy tents, O Jacob, thy dwellings O Israel"; 24:5

11. a. gold    b. silver    c. brass    d. iron e. tin  f. lead; 31:22

12. a. amulets b. bracelets    c. signet –rings    d. earrings    e. girdles; 31:50

13. a. drinking of wine, strong drink, or any grape derivative; 6:1-5b. no razor shall come upon his head; 6:5-6  c. he may not make himself unclean by contact with the dead, even for his own family; 6:6-9

14. a. if the people living in Canaan are strong or weak;    b. if the people are many or few, if there are trees or not;    c. if the land is good or bad, If the cities of the land or Canaan are walled or open; 13:17-21

15. a. Do not think you are the only holy one.    b. Why should you lift yourselves above the people.; 16:1-3

16. a. What to do with the gatherer of sticks on the Sabbath; 15:22    b. About the request of the daughters of Zelophechad; 36:1-10  c. What to do with those that were unable to celebrate the first Passover; 9:9

17. a. The almonds with the staff of Aaron; 17:24    b. The spies brought from Canaan; 13:23

18. a. Nadav   b. Avihu; 3:4

19. a. Eldad and Medad;    b. Who would (cause) that all the Lord's people were Prophets; 11:29

20. a. The king of Edom; 20:14    b. Sichon, king of the Amorites; 21:21

במדבר

21. Joshua, the son of Nun. Moses placed his hands on Joshua's head and gave him a charge; 27:15-23

# Match The Verses

1. "And shall not be reckoned among the nations"; 23:9

2. "And let mine end be like his"; 23:10

3. "And a scepter shall rise out of Israel"; 24:17

4. "And his kingdom shall be exalted"; 24:7

5. "Is for them like the horns of the wild ox"; 24:8

6. "Neither the son of man, that he should repent"; 23:19

7. "And numbered the stock of Israel"; 23:10

8. "Neither is there any divination"; 23:23

9. "I behold him but not high"; 24:17

10. "And his seed shall be in many waters"; 24:7

11. "But his end shall come to destruction"; 24:20

# Fill In The Missing Words

1. alone… reckoned; 23:9

2. war… here; 32:6

3. sin; 16:22

4. countenance… peace; 6:26

5. enemies; 10:35

6. guiltless; 32:22

7. sheep… shepherd; 27:17

8. princes… nobles; 21:18

9. soul… bread; 21:15

10. face… gracious; 6:25

11. meek… face; 12:3

12. people… prophets; 11:29

13. iniquities… greatness; 14:19

14. fringe… blue; 15:38

15. stranger… born; 9:14

16. enemies… scattered; 10:35

17. anger… loving kindness; 14:18

18. lioness… lion; 23:24

19. name… bless; 6:27

20. trumpets… peace offerings; 10:10

21. dough… gift; 15:21

22. bless… keep; 6:24

23. tents… dwellings; 24:5

# Identify The Relationship

1. The daughter; 26:46

2. The wife; 26:59

3. The grandson; 25:11

4. The father-in-law; 10:29

5. The uncle; 3:19

6. The brother; 3:2

7. The son: 1:7

8. The sister; 27:1

במדבר

9. The father; 16:1

10. The mother; 26:59

11. His father; 13:26

12. The son; 16:1

# Match The Place With The Event

1. There the Israelites sinned with the daughters of Moab; 25:1

2. Miriam became Leprous; 12:16

3. Miriam died there; 20:1-3

4. Where the Children of Israel lusted for meat; 11:34

5. Where Aaron died; 20:22-25

6. From where Moses saw Canaan; 27:12

7. The place of 12 springs of water; 33:9

8. The place from where the Children of Israel left Egypt; 33:3

# Identify The Names From The Descriptions

1. Balaam; 24:4

2. Zipporah; 12:1

3. Joshua; 11:28

4. The people of Moab; 21:29

5. The people of Hebron (the Giant); 13:22-29

6. Cozbi; 25:18

7. The king of Arad; 21:1

8. The straying wife; 5:22

9. Moses; 12:3

10. Joshua; 11:28

# Identify The Son

1. Balaam; 22:5

2. Moses; 26:59

3. Joshua; 13:8

4. Caleb; 13:6

במדבר

*Dr. Avital presents a prize to the winner of the National Bible Contest in May 1973. Seated to the right is Dr. Shlomo Kodesh, a world renowned Hebraist.*

# Answers and Sources
# For The Questions
# From Deuteronomy

# Multiple Choice

1. One year; 24:5

2. Sihon, king of Heshbon; 2:26

3. To go and serve other gods; 13:7

4. The witness 19:8-19

5. To the mitzvah of charity; 15:7

6. Women and horses; 17;16-17

7. Over one found slain in the field; 21:1

8. Wool and linen; 22:11

9. Great stones; 27:2

10. Asher;  33:24

11. By fleeing to a city of refuge; 19:4-5

12. To count seven weeks; 16:9

13. The third generation; 23:9

14. Moab; 1:5

15. Because God loved them; 7:6-8

16. Because they were strangers in the Land of Egypt: 10:19

17. An awl is thrust through his ear; 15:16-17

18. Because God gave them their lands as an inheritance; 2:5-9

19. Egypt; 11:10

20. The Elders; 21:6-7

21. At the bringing of the first-fruits; 26:1-5

22. A camel; 14:7

23. The Priest; 20:2

24. Twisted strings; 22:12

25. Moses; 34:7

26. Balaam; 23:6

27. A lost thing; 22:1-3

28. To the Kohen (the priest); 26:1

29. 120 years; 34:7

30. The same day; 24:15

31. Moses; 32:1

32. Joshua; 3:28

33. Sihon, King of Heshbon; 2:27

34. Two or three; 19:15

35. Those that are for food ; 20:19-20

36. a. Og, King of Bashan; 3:11

37. Fruit trees; 12:2-4

38. Three; 14:28-29

39. Leprosy; 24:8-9

40. King; 17:14

41. The blood; 12:23

42. Ox; 14:7

43. Double portion; 21:17

44. Thirty days; 34:8

45. Aviv; 16:1

46. Sukkot; 16:13

47. Horeb; 4:10

48. The Sea of the Arabah; 3:17

49. Wise men, full of knowledge; 1:13-15

50. Two and a half; 3:12-18

דברים

51. Nebo; 3:27-34

52. Joshua; 3:28

53. Three; 4:41-44

54. Mezuzah; 6:9

55. Forty days; 9:9

56. He threw down the tablets and broke them; 9:17

57. They worshipped their idols; 12:12

58. Prophet; 14:29

59. Rosh Hashanah; 16:16

60. He receives the same punishment that he sought to inflict; 19:16-19

61. When the sun goes down; 24:13

62. Menashe; 26:12-15

63. Horeb; 5:20-24

64. Asher; 33:24-25

65. Amorites; 1:44

66. Cities; 4:41-43

67. Parapet; 22:8

68. He is your brother; 23:8

69. His sandal; 25:5-10

70. Poverty; 37:3

71. Nuts; 8:8

72. Hermon; 3:10, 4:40

73. Gazelle; 14:3-8

74. Anyone who has a small child; 20:1-8

75. Aaron; 32:50

76. Shoes

# About Whom Or What Was It Said?

1. The tribe of Levi; 33:8

2. The tribe of Dan; 33:22

3. The king of Israel; 17:18

4. Lost property; 22:1-2

5. Ammon and Moab; 23:4-5

6. The second tithe; 26:13

7. The Torah; 30:12-13

8. The Hebrew slave; 15:14

9. Amalek; 25:17-18

10. The blood of an animal; 12:16

11. Tithe; 14:22-25

12. The gentile neighbors; 7:3-4

13. Blood avenger; 19:6

# Fill In The Missing Words

1. man…bread; 8:3

2. two…three; 17:6

3. lips…do; 23:24

4. Jeshurun…kicked; 32:15

5. cleave…alive; 4:4

6. declare…elders; 32:7

7. blind…wise; 16:19

8. alone…burden; 1:12

דברים

9. stranger…Egypt; 10:19

10. ox…threshing; 25:4

11. course…blessing; 23:6

12. bribes…blind; 16:19

13. fulfill…vowed; 23:24

14. secret…revealed; 29:28

15. comings…goings; 28:6

16. stubbornness…wickedness; 9:27

17. teaching…Moses; 4:44

18. one…seven; 28:7

19. heaven…earth; 30:19

20. God…rock; 32:15

21. iron…brass; 8:9

22. fathers…children; 24:16

## Identify The Following

1. Og; 3:11

2. Sihon; 2:30

3. Moses; 34:6

4. Machir; 3:15

5. The Hebrew slave; 15:16

6. Joshua; 3:28

7. Caleb; 1:36

8. Joseph; 33:17

9. Esau; 2:5

10. False prophet; 13:2

11. God; 10:17

12. Datan and Aviram; 11:6

13. Amalek; 25:17-19

14. Moab; 23:4-5

15. Moses; 9:9

16. The Children of Israel; 7:6

17. The tribe of Levi; 10:9

18. The tribe of Asher; 33:24

19. The tribe of Benjamin; 33:12

20. The tribe of Gad; 33:20

21. Joseph; 33:20

# Identify The Place

1. Where the curses were said; 27:13

2. The war with Og, king of Bashan; 3:1

3. Where the blessings were said; 27:12

4. Where Aaron died; 10:6

5. The spies took fruit of the land from there; 1:24-25

6. The land of Canaan; 1:28

7. Egypt; 4:20

8. Jericho; 34:3

9. Ar; 2:9

דברים

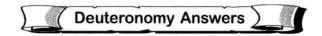

# Unique Questions

1. An animal that both chews it cud and has split hooves; 14:3-9

2. A fish that has both fins and scales; 14:3-9

3. Wheat, barley, grapes (wines), figs, pomegranates, olive trees, dates (honey)

4. a. All debts shall be released in the seventh year. b. Any Hebrew slave was free in the seventh year. c. The land was not cultivated during the seventh year; 15:1-8

5. By Moses to the Children of Israel in his last message to them before he died; 32:7

6. We are forbidden to destroy fruit trees because man eats from the tree, and also a tree is a living thing, as is man; 20: 19-20

7. a. "Honor thy father and mother"; 5:16   b. letting the mother bird of fledglings go free; 22:7   c. by having completely honest weights and measures; 25:15

8. Leket, shee-chah, pay-ah, peret, o'l'lot; 14:28-29; 24:19-21; 26:22 (Leviticus 19:9-10)

9. Because they attacked the Children of Israel without any reason during their journey from Egypt to Canaan; 25:17-19

10. a. You shall not plow with an ox and donkey together; 22:10   b. You shall not muzzle an ox while it is threshing; 25:4   c. You shall let the mother bird of fledglings go free; 22:6-7

11. a. Anyone who has not dedicated his newly-built house   b. Anyone who has not harvested his newly-planted vineyard   c. Anyone who is afraid; 20:5-8

12. He made an ark of acacia wood; 10:5

13. a. Bezer  b. Ramoth  c. Golan; 4:43

14. a. Vulture  b. Falcon  c. Raven  d. Ostrich  e) Owl  f) Stork  and others; 14:11-19

15. To prevent people from falling off of the roof; 22:8

16. They asked permission to pass through his land; 2:26-29

17. It is an abomination; 12:31

18. When chopping wood, the head of his axe slips off and kills a man; 19:5

19. It considers them an abomination; 18:9-12

20. He is returned to the place where he committed the crime and put to death; 19:11-13

21. The blessings were heard on Mount Grizim. The curses were heard on Mount Ebal; 11:29

22. Tefillin; 6:8

23. You must help him lift the donkey; 22:4

24. a. Because you were slaves in the land of Egypt   b. In order that your male or female slave shall rest as you do; 5:12-16

25. a. He cannot enter the house of the borrower   b. If the pledge is a night garment, he must return it before nightfall   c. If the pledge is a day garment, he must return it before daybreak; 14:9

26. a. The descendants of Esau who lived in Seir  b. the descendants of Lot and Moab; 2:4-19

27. a. Because they did not meet you with food and water on your journey after you left Egypt.   b. Because they hired Balaam, son of Beor from Pethor of Aram Naharaim, to curse you; 23:4-6

28. a. For he is your kinsman  b. For you were a stranger in his land; 23:8

29. The Shema – "Thou shalt love the Lord Thy God…"; 6:4

30. "Thou shalt not seethe a kid in its mother's milk"; 14:21

31. In the third part of the Shema, it says: "Speak to the Children of Israel, and bid them that they make them throughout their generations fringes in the corners of their garments, and that they put with the fringes of each corner a thread of blue"; 15:37-38

32. Reference is made in parts of the Torah to the enslavement of the Israelites in Egypt: "Love the stranger for you were strangers in the land of Egypt"; 10:19

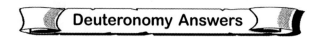

33. Tzedek, tzedek, tzedek (Hebrew) Justice, justice, justice shall you follow; 16:19-21

34. "A land of brooks, of water, of fountains and depths; a land of wheat and barley, and wines and fig trees and pomegranates; a land of olive trees and honey"; 8:7-9

35. It says: "Man does not live by bread alone"; 8:3

36. The Torah says: "For the poor shall never cease out of the land"; 15:11

37. The Torah instructs us: "His body shall not remain all night upon the tree" so that we do not defile the land; 21:23

38. "If you obey my commandments…I will grant the rain for your land in season…that you may gather your grain and wine and oil; 11:11-14

## Who Said What To Whom?

1. The spies to the Children of Israel; 1:25

2. Moses to Reuben and Gad and Menashe; 3:18

3. The officers to the people; 20:8

4. Moses to the Judges; 1:17

5. God to Moses; 9:14

6. The Levites to the Children of Israel; 27:25

7. Moses to Joshua; 31:6

8. Moses to the Children of Israel; 1:37

9. The bearer of the first fruits to the Priest; 26:3

10. To husband's brother by the widow; 25:9

11. God to Moses; 3:27

12. Moses to God; 3:25

דברים

*Dr. Avital leads the singing of "Hatikva" at the concluding assembly of the National Contest in New York in May 1978.*